THE CHARLES BABBAGE INSTITUTE

REPRINT SERIES FOR THE HISTORY OF COMPUTING

TITLES IN SERIES

1. *The Preparation of Programs for an Electronic Digital Computer* (1951), by Maurice V. Wilkes, David J. Wheeler, and Stanley Gill, 1984.

2. *Babbage's Calculating Engines: A Collection of Papers* (1889), by Henry Prevost Babbage, 1984.

3. *Handbook of the Napier Tercentenary Celebration or Modern Instruments and Methods of Calculation* (1914), edited by E. M. Horsburgh, 1984.

4. *High-Speed Computing Devices* (1950), by Engineering Research Associates, Inc., 1984.

5. *Punched Card Methods in Scientific Computation* (1940), by W. J. Eckert, 1984.

6. *Calculating Machines: Recent and Prospective Developments and Their Impact on Mathematical Physics* (1947) and *Calculating Instruments and Machines* (1949), by Douglas R. Hartree, F.R.S., 1984.

7. *Proceedings of a Symposium on Large-Scale Digital Calculating Machinery* (1947), jointly sponsored by The Navy Department Bureau of Ordnance and The Harvard University Computation Laboratory, 1985.

8. *A Manual of Operation for the Automatic Sequence Controlled Calculator* (1946), by The Harvard University Computation Laboratory, 1985.

9. *The Moore School Lectures* (1946), edited by Martin Campbell-Kelly and Michael R. Williams, 1985.

10. *A. M. Turing's ACE Report of 1946 and Other Reports*, edited by B. E. Carpenter and R. W. Doran, 1986.

11. *Le Calcul Simplifié: Graphical and Mechanical Methods for Simplifying Calculation* (based on 3rd ed., 1928), by Maurice d'Ocagne, translated by J. Howlett and M. R. Williams, 1986.

LE CALCUL SIMPLIFIÉ

Graphical and Mechanical Methods for Simplifying Calculation

VOLUME 11

IN THE

CHARLES BABBAGE INSTITUTE

REPRINT SERIES FOR THE

HISTORY OF COMPUTING

THE CHARLES BABBAGE INSTITUTE REPRINT SERIES FOR THE HISTORY OF COMPUTING

This volume is one of a series of works selected for reprinting by an editorial board of the Charles Babbage Institute. The Charles Babbage Institute for the History of Information Processing was founded in late 1977 to promote study of the technical and socioeconomic aspects of the development of information processing. To this end, the Institute serves as an archive of the history of information processing; as a clearinghouse for information about historical material and interested persons; and as a foundation that fosters research and writing in the field of information processing through the use of historical materials. In 1980 the Institute moved to its permanent home at the University of Minnesota.

The principal aim of the reprint series has been to make the key literature of the history of computing more accessible. Until now, the scarcity of many significant works has been a handicap to serious study. Reprinted items include classic textbooks, influential reports, and conference proceedings that have proved to be significant steps in the development of the subject. If original editing or print quality now seems unsatisfactory, new editions of some works are to be offered. In addition, non-English works are translated. Most volumes are provided with an authoritative introduction to afford insight and context for the present-day reader.

In selecting works for reprinting, the editorial board has consciously endeavored to produce a balanced collection of material that is representative of the full spectrum of the history of computing. The complete series will thus form a sound basis for studies in the history of computing, and will be of value both to active historians and to computer practitioners interested in the origins of their subject.

Maurice d'Ocagne, 1862–1938. (Photograph courtesy of the Bibliothèque Centrale, École Polytechnique.)

Le Calcul Simplifié

Graphical and Mechanical Methods for Simplifying Calculation

Maurice d'Ocagne

translated by
J. Howlett and
M. R. Williams

The MIT Press
Cambridge, Massachusetts
London, England

and

Tomash Publishers
Los Angeles/San Francisco

Publisher's Note

This book is a translation of the third edition of *Le Calcul Simplifié* by Maurice d'Ocagne, published by Gauthier-Villars in Paris in 1928.

This book was set in Times New Roman by Asco Trade Typesetting Ltd., Hong Kong, and printed and bound by Halliday Lithograph in the United States of America.

Library of Congress Cataloging-in-Publication Data

Ocagne, Maurice d', 1862–1938.
Le calcul simplifié.

(Charles Babbage Institute reprint series for the history of computing; 11)
Translation of: Calcul simplifié par les procédés mécaniques et graphiques.
Bibliography: p.
Includes index.
1. Calculators. 2. Mathematical instruments. 3. Graphic methods.
I. Title. II. Series. QA75.01513 1986 510'.285 85-23297
ISBN 0-262-15032-8

New Introduction for This Edition

The Book

This volume marks a significant point in the publishing program of the Charles Babbage Institute Reprint Series for the History of Computing. It is the eleventh volume to appear in this series, but the first that had to be translated into English. This fact alone should make it an interesting volume to scholars who now have material that had previously been difficult to obtain.

Le Calcul Simplifié is a classic work on the art of computation. It was initially written, in the early 1890s, at a time before commercial mechanical calculating machines were readily available. It gives a very good feeling for just how primitive the calculating aids were during that era and how much effort was devoted to solving problems that today would be considered trivial. Not only was a great deal of thought put into devising sophisticated calculating devices such as nomograms, but the considerable ingenuity shown in the engineering of mechanical calculators deserves our highest admiration. Both of these intriguing aspects of calculation are dealt with, in depth, in this volume.

The book spans the range from the simplest and most trivial arithmetic instruments to the very complex mechanical motions needed in the Scheutz difference machine. Along the way d'Ocagne gives us a tour through all the known forms of mechanical calculators, the integraphs and planimeters, the different kinds of nomograms, and the mechanical implementation of some nomographic ideas.

Chapter I presents us with a taxonomy of mechanical calculators that was the first to classify this field of knowledge in a way that is still valid today. It is quite obvious that d'Ocagne was not a shy individual because he takes great pains to point out that this classification scheme was his own invention and that before he arrived on the scene all was chaos. Although this is only one of many places in this volume where d'Ocagne seems concerned to ensure his correct place in history, he usually does it where it is properly justified. Earlier descriptions of mechanical calculating machines were usually lacking in any form or structure and, as a consequence, were a great deal more confusing than the one put forward here.

Although Chapters II and III ("Graphical Calculation" and "Grapho-Mechanical Calculation") are interesting in their own right, they really act as an introduction to the much more detailed content of Chapter IV: "Nomographic Calculation." Here d'Ocagne was on home ground. He was considered the founder and world expert in this field. Again, he seldom lets us forget the place he holds, particularly in the endnotes that are often used to justify his own priority of invention.

The subject of nomography, and its continuation in Chapter V as "Nomo-Mechanical Calculation," is not particularly easy to understand. Individual nomograms were usually easy to use for a particular calculation, but the underlying fundamental concepts can be very abstruse. The uninitiated reader would do best to skim through the text of these chapters, noting the diagrams and nomographic examples, and only then returning to a careful examination of d'Ocagne's descriptions of ideas such as "doubly numbered points making contact with singly numbered lines." The description, while not easy, is one of the most complete in existence and, together with the references in the endnotes, constitutes a resource that future historians should find useful.

The one other great resource in this volume is the description in Appendix I of Tchebichef's[1] calculating machine. As far as the editors are aware, this is the only full description that exists of this complex device. At first sight this description, like that for nomograms, appears very difficult to follow. Initially, the editors could not help but wonder why very much simpler terminology, such as that found in the manuals for Brunsviga calculators, was not employed in the "Instructions for Use of the Machine." A few minutes thought, however, reminded us that Tchebichef produced this device before the Brunsviga machines were designed. The fact that, as we point out in endnotes at appropriate places, this section may well have been initially inspired, if not actually written, by Tchebichef himself may well account for some of the rather pedantic nature of the description and explanation.

It remains an unsolved problem as to how much effect, if any, the Tchebichef machine had on the design of the subsequent commercially produced calculators. The device itself still sits, rather forlornly, in a glass case at the Conservatoire des Arts et Métiers. If any attempt has been made to indicate its relevance, it is not apparent from the simple label and lack of explanatory material shown by its present owners.

The Author

Maurice d'Ocagne was born in Paris in 1862. He spent most of his working life in various positions with the French government or academic institutes.

Starting with an appointment as an engineer in the Corps de Ponts et Chaussées from 1885 to 1889, he moved and spent several years working on hydrological problems around Cherbourg, became a Professor at the École Nationale des Ponts et Chaussées in 1894, was appointed Director General of the French mapping service in 1901, appointed to the post of Professor at the École Polytechnique in 1912, became Inspector General of the Ponts et Chaussées in 1920, and a member of the prestigious Académie des Sciences in 1922. These appointments, unlike some similar titles in other countries, were not political patronage posts but were important technical positions given to only the most able individuals. The d'Ocagne name is little known today, but both the man and his work were highly regarded in the days before the sophisticated mechanical desk calculator, and the later electronic devices, displaced the use of his major development, the nomogram.

Although d'Ocagne's main interest was in the field of nomography, his *Traité de Nomographie* being considered the fundamental and classic work in the field, he kept himself informed as to the state of the art in almost all other fields that had an impact on the physical process of performing calculations. As a result, this book presents a picture of, and comparison between, almost all possible devices and methods of performing calculation just before the explosive growth that was introduced into the field by complex mechanical, electrical, and electronic devices.

Translation and Editing

The editors have chosen to work with the third (1928) edition of *Le Calcul Simplifié*, not because it contained more information than the earlier editions, but because it was slightly better organized, with some scattered material gathered together in the form of appendixes, than the two earlier editions. This last edition also took advantage of some developments that took place during the First World War, particularly noticeable in references to nomograms for solving problems in ballistics, to bring the material up to date. This updating for the third edition necessitated that d'Ocagne either condense or eliminate entirely the discussion of very outdated machines. Examples of this type of revision include the very much shortened description of the workings of various cash registers and the entire elimination of several pages devoted to explaining the workings of Leibniz's calculating machine—an elimination that the present editors had to overcome by inserting an extra diagram to help the reader make sense of the explanation that d'Ocagne did provide.

Another reason for wanting to republish the third edition is that, because of the very high acid content of the paper and bindings, all copies known to the editors are in very poor physical condition. The pages are yellowed and brittle, and the bindings are never in good enough shape to allow the books to be opened and used freely without danger of damage.

Although improved in organization, it has to be admitted that the layout and typography of the third edition was inferior to that used in the second (1905) edition. We have also attempted to correct this by adopting what we hope is a more pleasing typeface and page layout.

The 1928 French edition of this work was *very* difficult to read in places. Not only does the book, by its very nature, contain some archaic and obscure terms, but d'Ocagne seemed to delight in producing paragraphs of several hundred words, all of which were contained in one single sentence. Even when long paragraphs consisted of several sentences, it was often the case that they would include such errors as ambiguous punctuation, closing brackets with no corresponding opening ones, and even the occasional sentence that failed to contain a verb. This meant that a "word-for-word" translation was completely out of the question. There were even occasions when whole sections of the work were written in such an ambiguous style that the editors came to question whether d'Ocagne might not have done it purposefully in order to cover up the fact that he was not completely familiar with some particular mechanism.

We have, none the less, attempted to stick as closely as possible to the flavor and spirit of the language used in the original edition. For example, we have preserved d'Ocagne's style of emphasis by the use of italics as far as the limits of translation would allow. Any deviation from d'Ocagne's original was usually done for a good reason—usually the fact that, at that point, the original wording simply did not make sense. The editors have been very careful to indicate where substantive changes (usually to correct an error) have been made by attaching an endnote at that point. All endnotes that were not in the d'Ocagne original are flagged as such by the prefix (Ed.). The text between this editorial flag and the end of the note is the work of the present editors; all other notes are from the original text.

The original notes were true footnotes, being placed at the feet of the pages in which they were referenced. This made for a very distracting format, the footnotes occasionally requiring more space on a page than the main text. As they are mainly references or explanations of fine points that seldom add much in the way of immediate information, we have taken the editorial decision to gather them together as endnotes appearing after the chapters in which the references occur.

The figures and diagrams retain the same numbers as in the original text. Whenever the editors deemed it necessary to introduce an extra diagram in order to avoid a problem with the main text, it was always given the same number as the immediately preceding figure with an additional letter designation. For example: *Figure 11* was in the original text, while *Figure 11a* has been added by the editors. Editorial endnotes have also been added to the text in order further to flag these as additions to the original. Although the same numbering scheme has been kept, it was necessary to make slight changes to the placement of the figures in the text to accommodate the needs of the new typesetting format. In all cases these changes are minimal and should not be of concern to either the historian or general reader.

The Index, which in d'Ocagne's text was simply a list of names of people mentioned in the book, has been expanded slightly to aid in finding specific topics. It still consists largely of a list of surnames taken almost intact from the original and thus more closely resembles an unstructured shopping list than a proper book Index. The author had a peculiar habit of referring to people simply be their surname (e.g., Smith) with no initials or other identifying information. Occasionally he would add some indication of a person's military rank or country or origin. It is often possible to determine the initials of the people by reference to the Index, where he occasionally includes this information, or by checking the Bibliography, where he uses the full form of an author's name. Rather than adding this information to the main text, we decided to continue with d'Ocagne's style and use only the surname unless he specifically mentioned first names or initials.

The translation of particularly obscure phrases has been a slight problem. In these cases we attempted to contact experts in the field to obtain guidance as to the proper English terminology. Although every attempt has been made to keep to the original spirit, translation errors will have occurred; we can but hope that the reader will forgive us and enjoy the remaining sections of the work. We found it fascinating and can vouch for the fact that a careful study of d'Ocagne's work will result in a deeper understanding of the art of computation.

Note

1. The name Tchebichef is also transliterated as Tchebicheff, Tchebycheff, or Chebyshev. We have kept d'Ocagne's transliteration because, as he indicated in note 1 to Appendix I, Tchebichef himself preferred this particular version.

September 23, 1985
J. Howlett, Oxford
M. R. Williams, Calgary

Maurice d'Ocagne in his student days at the École Polytechnique.
(Photograph courtesy of the Bibliothèque Centrale, École Polytechnique.)

Le Calcul Simplifié

OR

Graphical and Mechanical Methods for Simplifying Calculation

A General Outline
Covering
Mechanical, Graphical, Grapho-Mechanical,
Nomographic, and Nomo-Mechanical Methods

by

Maurice d'Ocagne
Member of the Institute
Professor at the École Polytechnique

Third Edition
completely revised with many additions

LE

CALCUL SIMPLIFIÉ

PAR LES

PROCÉDÉS MÉCANIQUES ET GRAPHIQUES

ESQUISSE GÉNÉRALE

COMPRENANT :

CALCUL MÉCANIQUE. — CALCUL GRAPHIQUE
CALCUL GRAPHOMÉCANIQUE
CALCUL NOMOGRAPHIQUE. — CALCUL NOMOMÉCANIQUE

PAR

Maurice d'OCAGNE

MEMBRE DE L'INSTITUT
PROFESSEUR A L'ÉCOLE POLYTECHNIQUE

TROISIÈME ÉDITION
avec une rédaction entièrement renouvelée et de nombreuses additions

PARIS
GAUTHIER-VILLARS ET Cie, IMPRIMEURS LIBRAIRES
DU BUREAU DES LONGITUDES, DE L'ÉCOLE POLYTECHNIQUE
Quai des Grands-Augustins, 55

1928

Table of Contents

Foreword to the Third Edition

The first edition of this book simply reproduced the course of lectures given at the Conservatoire des Arts et Métiers in 1893, the aim of which was to give a consolidated picture of the possibilities for simplifying calculation offered by geometry and mechanical engineering. Much additional material was presented in the second edition, published in 1905, but the general plan remained unchanged.

Since that time, however, there have been considerable developments, on the one hand in geometrical and mechanical methods of calculation and, on the other, in our attitude toward the subject as a whole. These have led us to a complete rewriting of the book, for this third edition, rather than a mere revision of the earlier material. In this rewriting we have held to the classification of the subject matter that we gave in our paper to the Académie des Sciences in January 1926 (*C.R.* Vol. 182, p. 191), the principles of which we summarize in the Introduction that follows. It is a consequence of this classification that we felt it necessary to include something on graphical and grapho-mechanical methods of integration, a topic omitted from the earlier editions.

As our aim in writing this book has been only to describe the essential features of the various methods available for simplifying calculation, we have sought to give it that character of a first introduction to, and popularization of, these methods. We have therefore left the details, whether technical or mathematical, to specialist works to which the present book can be regarded as a general introduction. Many points of detail are dealt with in reference *6* of the Bibliography at the end of the present volume, which itself has a very extensive bibliography.

Two topics dealt with in notes in the second edition are here presented as appendixes. These are Tchebichef's calculating machine, our account of which was written in the presence of the distinguished inventor himself and which is the only existing detailed description of this machine, and the ingenious method for representing the action of certain difference machines due to Engineer-Colonel Bertrand.

Our grateful thanks are due to Mr. Jean Vèzes, a former student of ours at the École Polytechnique, for his invaluable help with the revision of the chapter on arithmetical machines. Mr. Vèzes is now one of the leading experts in this branch of precision mechanics; he has shown us his plan for the *Traité Général des Machines à Calculer*, which he is currently writing. This should be the most complete and most scholarly work ever published on the subject.[1] A full treatment of the *comparative anatomy of calculating machines* will be given, the foundations of which we laid out in the first edition of this present work and of which a more detailed account, although still in summary form, is given in this third edition.[2]

Our thanks are due also to another expert in the field of instruments of calculation, Mr. Lucien Malassis. While he is not a professional in this field, he has become well known both for the ingenious devices he has invented and for his remarkable collection of objects and documents related to it.

Notes

1. (Ed.) The editors can find no record to indicate that this work was ever published in a usable form.

2. References ***16*** and ***18*** give a more or less complete list of existing machines, but neither makes any attempt at a rational classification.

Introduction

1: On the General Value of Simplifying Calculation

The importance of calculation is evident in both the theoretical and the practical realms. The material progress achieved by our civilization is derived more or less directly from Science, and Science itself cannot progress without the constant support of calculation. Moreover, calculation is not only a concern in what are traditionally known as the *exact* sciences such as Mechanics and Astronomy, in which it plays an essential role, but also in those that even recently have been considered as only experimental or observational sciences; this arises as a consequence of the greater use of more precise methods brought about by modern developments.

In all branches of Physics, and even in Chemistry, the mathematical formula has come to be of major importance. Physiology too may make equal use of this since the need has been recognized to introduce the idea of measurement into the study of the facts concerning this subject.

Thus, more than ever before, we can say with Plato that *numbers rule the world.* But in general, as has often been said, they may rule the world but their government is not appreciated.

General Menabrea, a mathematician well known in Paris because of the fact that he held the position of Italian Ambassador for several years, wrote the following lines:[1]

> How many precious observations have remained unused in furthering the progress of science because there was not the power to calculate their results! What weight of discouragement has the prospect of a long and exhausting calculation cast on the soul of the man of genius, who asks only the time to think but sees this devoured by this work! And yet it is by the hard road of analysis that he will reach the truth; but he cannot follow this road unless guided by numbers, for without numbers he is not given the power to lift the veil behind which are hidden the mysteries of nature.

While calculation is an indispensible aid to scientific research, it is also the tool through which the principles discovered by this research are brought into practical use. Thus it is that the navigator, the surveyor, the artilleryman, the mechanic, the electrician, the financier, and the engineer must always be making use of these principles and for each of them calculation is an important part, and certainly not the least arduous part, of the daily work. Simplification of calculation will relieve each worker of much of his burden. Sometimes it may do even more by making possible, or even easy, a task that would otherwise have demanded an effort disproportunate to the result to be obtained and one that no one, perhaps, would be willing to make.

This last statement has not, of course, taken into account the famous exceptions for whom it would not be true. We know that in some individuals the power of calculation can reach such a level that they must be regarded as prodigies.

2: A Few Words on Calculating Prodigies

The names of a few calculating prodigies are preserved in the history of calculation; for example:[2]

- The young Mathieu Le Coq, from Lorraine, who in Florence at the age of 8 astonished Balthasar de Monconys during the latter's third journey to Italy (1664).
- Mrs. de Lingré, who in the salons of the Restoration, according to Mrs. Genlis,[3] carried out the most complicated operations in her head while surrounded by the noise of conversation.
- The negro slave Tom Fuller, of Virginia, who died toward the end of the 18th century, aged 80, without having learned to read or write.
- The Wurtemburg shepherd Dinner.
- The Tyrolean shepherd Pierre Annich.
- The Englishman Jeddediah[4] Buxton, a simple corn thresher.
- The American Zerah Colburn, who was in succession an actor, a Methodist deacon, and a language teacher.
- Dase, for whom calculation was his only faculty, and which he applied to continue Burckhardt's tables of prime factors to numbers between 7,000,000 and 10,000,000.
- Bidder, builder of the Victoria Docks in London, who became President of the Institution of Civil Engineers and who passed on some of his calculating gifts to his son George.
- The Scicilian shepherd Vito Mangiamelle, who also had great skill in learning languages.
- The young Pughiesi from Piedmont.
- The Russians Ivan Petroff and Mikail Cerebriakof.[5]
- The shepherd Henri Mondeux, from Touraine, who was very popular during the reign of Louis-Philippe.
- The young Prolongeau from Bordeaux.

- Grandemange, born with neither arms nor legs.[6]
- Vinckler, who was the subject of a remarkable experiment conducted at Oxford University.[7]

The author has, himself, been present at a wonderful display of calculating powers given by Jacques Inaudi, from Piedmont, who also was originally a shepherd and who has found one of similar powers in the person the Greek Diamandi.[8] Finally, a calculator of the same order of skill has appeared very recently in the person of the Spaniard Sanmartin, who was the subject of an experiment at the Madrid Academy of Sciences.[9] One cannot fail to be struck by the number of these extraordinary calculators who spent their childhood tending sheep. For them, calculation was at first a way of passing the time so as to relieve the boredom of long hours spent in the middle of the fields.

While such powers of calculation are extremely rare, they are not usually accompanied by a comparable development of other faculties. It seems that the brain, fully absorbed by such a function, is scarcely able to vary its activities. It is a misconception, although a very common one, to confuse great skill in calculation with special gifts in mathematics.[10] Neither intuition nor logic, which play the leading roles in the mathematical sciences, is necessarily related to facility in mental arithmetic, which makes demands only on memory. To confuse the two is to make the same mistake as considering exceptional manual skill at the piano keyboard to indicate an outstanding gift for musical composition. Nevertheless there have been mathematicians who were also skilful calculators, among the most famous of whom were Wallis, Euler, Gauss, and Ampère.

Although one should never rely on such generalizations, it can be said with confidence that every simplification brought about in numerical calculation constitutes truly general progress. It relieves workers of some of the boredom and weariness associated with calculation, reduces the loss of time that calculation involves, and also reduces the chance of mistakes.

3: The Role of Tables in Numerical Calculation

Counting one unit at a time in order to progress from one number to the next in the sequence of natural integers is the basis on which all numerical calculation rests. Practical calculations are being reduced ever more closely to this operation by means of numerical tables. Counting made it possible to construct first an addition table for pairs of numbers and, subsequently, multiplication tables. Using these, other tables could then be constructed. Assuming that the two primary tables are continued to the limit of the numbers encountered in practice, the result of any addition or multiplication (and, by an inverse process, of any subtraction or division) can be found without the need to perform any of these operations. The operations that have to be used in applying the known rules of elementary arithmetic have no other aim but to limit the use of the addition and multiplication tables to the parts concerning numbers of only single digits. Since, as children, we learn these reduced tables by heart, we have the ability to perform any calculation without the need to have any table before us. However, as multiplications often have to be performed on large numbers, very extended tables have been produced. An example would be Crelle's tables, which give the product by each single digit of all integers not exceeding 10,000,000.[11]

It was with the aim of providing multiplication tables that would be useful over a wide range, yet be of small physical dimensions, that John Napier, Baron of Merchiston,[12] conceived of an ingenious device. This illustrious inventor of logarithms had the idea of making the various columns of the multiplication table movable so as to be able to put them side by side in the order of the digits of the multiplicand and, further, of dividing each square into two parts by a diagonal so as to separate the tens digit from the units. To use this device to find the product of any number by a single digit, say 365 times 7, arrange the colums for 0, 3, 6, and 5 (in that order) as shown in *Figure 1*. The column for 0 contains the multipliers from 1 to 9 engraved in each box.

Against the Figure 7 of column 0 are the 7th multiples of the digits of the multiplicand. All that is needed is to add the tens digit in each square to the

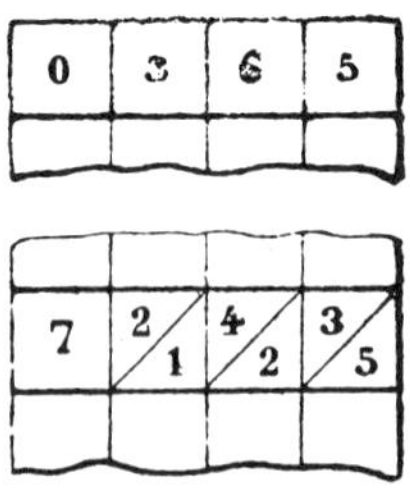

Figure 1

units digit in the neighboring square, that is, to add *parallel to the diagonals*, in order to have the required product, 2555.

Napier described this method in his *Rabdologia*, published in Edinburgh in 1617, and produced it in a practical form in his *Prompturarium*.[13] It is certain that he owed the idea to no one; but it is interesting to note that the method for performing multiplication taught by the 15th-century Arabian mathematician Alkalcadi, and found in the *Arithmetic* of Peter Apian (1593), is based on the same principle as Napier's rods.

In order to conform to more standard usage, an arrangement can be made in which the additions are made vertically. All that is necessary is to replace the vertical columns by columns inclined at 45 degrees, as in *Figure 2*.

It should be noted that with the simple division of the multiplication table into nine movable columns, only numbers in which no two digits are equal can be represented. The number columns that may be used can be increased by using rods of square cross section with a different column inscribed on each of the four faces. It is still better, as was proposed by the Jesuit Gaspard Schott in his *Organum Mathematicum* (1688), to replace the rods by parallel cylinders whose surfaces are divided into ten bands numbered 0 to 9, giving the nine columns of the Pythagorean table plus a column for 0. An illustration from Schott's work is reporduced as *Figure 2a*.[14]

Schott's proposal has been put forward again several times since then, in particular by Grillet, clockmaker to the King (1678),[15] and by Hélie (1839).[16]

Petit (1671)[17] proposed a scheme in which Napier's bones took the form

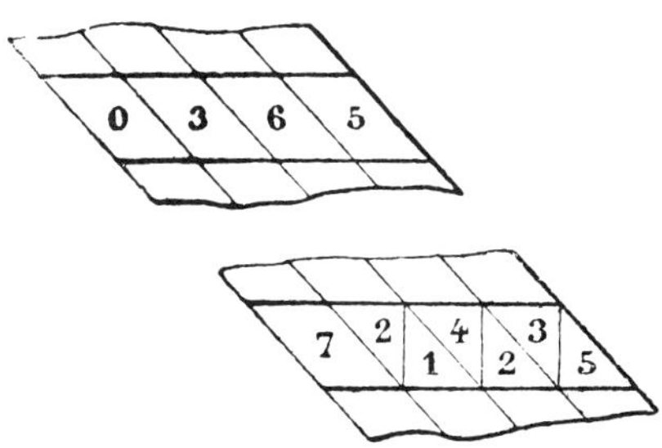

Figure 2

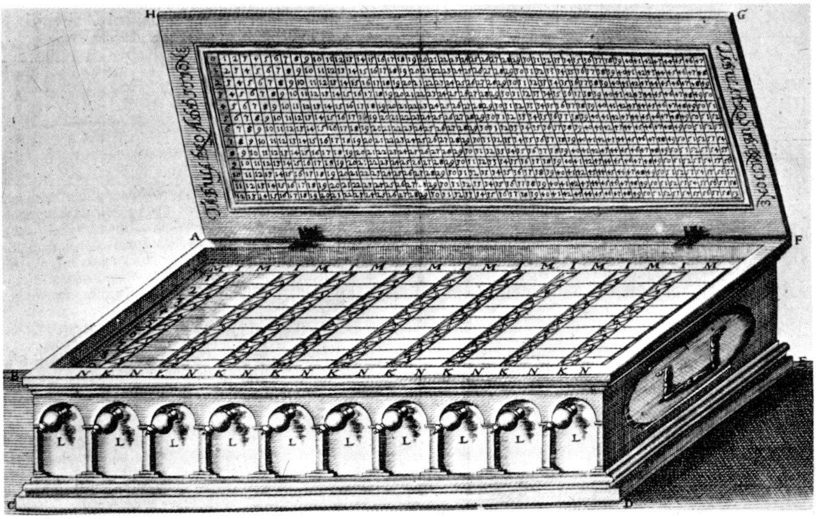

Figure 2a

of circular disks revolving on a cylindrical drum, and Leupold (1727)[18] built a similar apparatus in which a number of decagonal disks could move with respect to one another. Poetius (1728)[19] in his *Mensula Pythagorica* gave them the form of concentric circles, with variations proposed by Prahl (1789) (called *arithmetica portatilis*), and by Gruson (1790).

In addition to Napier's own modification of the bones, which he called *Promptuararium*, interested readers should note the works of Reyher (1688), Méan (1731),[20] Roussain (1738),[21] Jordans (1797), Bardach (1839), Lapeyre (1840), Dubois (1861),[22] E. Bec (1911),[23] and A. Noury (1919).[24] In the systems proposed by Roussain and Doubois different colors are used to help differentiate the rows.[25] Colonel Quinement arranged Napier's bones into concentric circles, each movable with respect to one another, so that the partial products to be added together could be read along a radius. Pouvost-le-Guay,[26] whose arrangement of the bones was published in Paris in 1890, simplified their use significantly by having the rods joined together in pairs.

During the printing of this book the author became aware of a new instrument for performing multiplication, designed by Mr. Thibout of the Catholic Institute of Angers. It uses rods similar to Napier's, manipulated by a very simple and ingenious device.[27]

Napier's bones are able to give products of any number times a single digit, but only at a cost of the user performing intermediate additions of two single-digit integers. The next advance was to create a device that removed the need for even this small amount of work.

In 1841 Dr. Roth, whose name is associated with several arithmetical inventions, conceived a device that came close to realizing this aim. His apparatus[28] contained a number of slots through which the digits of the product could be viewed. Some of these digits were printed in black and others in red; the black ones were to be taken as they stood, while the red ones were to be increased by one before being written down as part of the product. While this was certainly an advance on the purely Naperian procedure, it was possible to go further in this direction. The next improvement was done by Genaille,[29] an engineer with the French State Railways, whose version of the bones was demonstrated at the Congrès de l'Association Française pour l'Avancement de Sciences by Édouard Lucas in 1885.

As a result of a careful study of the formation of the products in Napier's bones, Genaille saw that these could be obtained by means of numbered scales engraved on each of ten rods (numbered 0, 1, 2, . . . , 9) between which the eye was guided by a sequence of arrows engraved on the rods. Each rod has four faces and, if the engravings for a different digit were placed on each face, then a set of ten rods would allow any six-digit multiplicand (having up to four identical digits) to be used.

The arrangement in *Figure 3* indicates how Genaille's rules are used to multiply 42,457 by 8.

The leftmost rod, corresponding to the digit 0, is fixed on the lid of the box and the rods for the digits 4, 2, 4, 5, 7 are then arranged beside it as shown, with the horizontal lines being carefully aligned. To find the 8th multiple of 42,457, start with the upper right-hand digit in the 8th row (i.e. the 6 in this case) and follow the dark arrows to the left, reading off each digit as it is encountered. In this case the device gives, in succession, 6, 5, 6, 9, 3, 3 and the product (339, 656) is found by a simple reading process. It is much easier to perform this operation than to explain it and its simplicity is such that, as I myself have seen, a young child who has not yet learned the multiplication table can be asked to multiply a six-digit number by a single digit and perform it without error.[30]

Genaille also made use of cylinders, similar to those of Schott described earlier, so as to be able to deal with any number, regardless of the number of

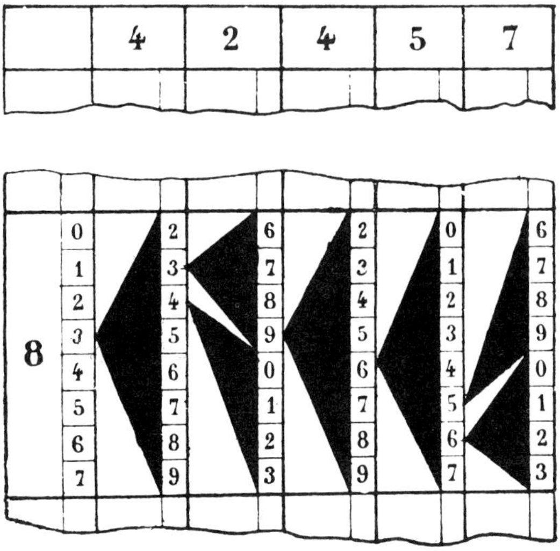

Figure 3

identical digits it may have. Presume that we have 20 such cylinders placed side by side; we would then have a device that would give us all the 1st, 2nd, 3rd, ..., 9th multiples of all numbers less than 100,000,000,000,000,000,000—the hundred quintillionth![31]

Genaille devised similar rules for division and for calculating daily interest, correct to a thousandth of a franc, on any capital sum invested at the usual rates.[32]

Starting from the fundamental tables for addition and multiplication, other tables can be constructed for special calculations. It is possible to simplify the calculations needed to make these tables in order to reduce greatly the amount of work that would be required if every entry had to be calculated directly. The main method used to simplify table creation is what mathematicians call the *calculus of differences*.[33] A typical example will show the type of help that can be expected from this method of calculation.

Suppose we wish to calculate a table of squares of the natural numbers, to be arranged in two columns with one containing the numbers 1, 2, 3, ..., and the other their squares 1, 4, 9, ... If we do this by taking each number in succession and multiplying it by itself we shall soon recoil from the length and tediousness of the calculations. The calculus of differences comes to our aid by offering the following solution: we add, temporarily, a third column to the table, in which we write the sequence of odd numbers starting with 3; each square in the second column is then obtained from its predecessor by the simple addition of the odd number in the third column to its adjacent square, producing the following table:

Numbers	Squares	Differences
1	1	3
2	4	5
3	9	7
4	16	9
5	25	11
⋮	⋮	⋮

The property of differences, shown here in the construction of a table of squares, extends to much more general cases. Note that the difference between the successive differences that we have used (the odd numbers) is constant and equal to 2. We say that the *second difference of the squares of the integers is constant*, and it is in this form that the proposition is generalized. If instead of a simple square we consider a polynomial of second degree,

$$AX^2 + BX + C,$$

and, if instead of increasing the number x (called the *argument* of the table) from 1 by 1 at each step, we start the table at any value and increase it by a constant, the table will still have a constant second difference.

The property of a constant second difference for polynomials of second degree generalizes for the 3rd, 4th, ..., nth degree polynomials, the only change being that it is then the 3rd, 4th, ..., nth differences that are constants. We shall see later how special machines can help[34] in performing calculations of this type.

When the results to be calculated depend on a single variable, as in the table of squares, the sequence of values of the *argument* are written in the first column and the corresponding results (the values of the function) in the second column adjacent to the first. We then have a *single-entry table* or *simple barème*,[35] after the French calculator Barrême (1640–1703), who was the first to apply tables of this kind to frequently needed calculations. These tables were described in his *Livre de Comptes Faits* (1670), which remains, justly, popular.[36]

Tables of functions with two variables are constructed such that the values of the variables are written, in increasing order, along one line at the head of the table and the other in a column at the side. Each result is written at the intersection of the row and column corresponding to the values of the two variables used in the calculation. This results in what is known as a *double-entry table* or *double barème*.[37] Various simplifications in the calculational procedures used to produce such tables can be made, similar to those described for simple barèmes; however, there is no need to say more on this point.

In 1872, because of the importance of numerical tables in all applications of the mathematical sciences, the *British Association for the Advancement of Science* set up a *Committee on Mathematical Tables*[38] to compile as complete a catalogue as possible of the tables then in existence and to reprint or calculate such tables as they consider necessary. The first, very extensive, report was presented to the Association in 1873 and this was followed by several others in 1878, 1883, etc.

We shall not go into detail on this subject but will only give a short account of certain arrangements that have been made, in response to practical needs, to reduce the size of tables. These have transformed tables into a kind of calculating device. Two devices, in the collection of the Conservatoire des Arts et Métiers, developed by Mrs. Didelin and Chambon, respectively, will serve as examples.

Mr. Didelin's device enables the daily interest to be calculated on a capital sum of any value up to 100,000 francs (Fr.) at the usual rates, going in steps of 0.25, to 7%, as well as for 8% and 9%. If these results were given in the form of a single-entry table with thirty columns, one for each interest rate, a total of 100,000 lines would be needed. However, any sum can be broken down into hundreds of thousands, tens of thousands, . . . , tens, and units. If the separate interests for these different parts are available, their sum will give the interest required. Thus the table can be reduced to one of 45 lines, corresponding to:

1	2	3	· · ·	9
10	20	30	· · ·	90
·	·	·	· · ·	·
10,000	20,000	30,000	· · ·	90,000

plus one line for 100,000.

The first line of nine entries is written on the surface of a cylinder, the second line on another cylinder placed alongside the first, and so on to the fifth, which contains the entries for the tens of thousands plus the line corresponding to 100,000. If this set of cylinders is covered with a sheet, cut with longitudinal windows through which the uppermost generator of each cylinder can be seen, all that has to be done in order to find the required interest is to turn the cylinder so as to bring the entry corresponding to the required digit under the window and then to add together the numbers thus seen.[39]

This arrangement of numerical table on adjacent cylinders has the further advantage of being extendable to certain tables having three entries. It is clear that, if by some means the numbers read from the cylinders can be made to vary according to the values of a third entry, then a *triple barème* has been achieved. It is this idea that Mr. Chambon most ingeniously put into practice in his *Calculateur d'intérêts*, which gives the interest payable, for any number of days, on capital sums up to 99,999 Fr. at rates of 3, 3.5, 4, 4.5, 5, 5.5, and 6%. The vertical columns of the table correspond to the first entry, the number of days. As in the Didelin device, the units, tens, . . . , tens of thousands are assigned to the various cylinders, on each of which an endless loop contains the nine lines corresponding to the second entry.

Although Chambon's arrangement is most ingenious, and most appropriate to the particular application for which it was developed, it does not allow any great increase in the number of distinct values for the third entry; consequently its use is rather limited.

Triple-entry tables are not, in practice, capable of any significant extension, and there is really no case for even considering tables of more than three entries. Must we, therefore, resign ourselves to forgoing the great benefits that such calculated tables can give, when these would involve more than two variables? Fortunately for us this is not the case, thanks to a special way of using graphical methods that provides powerful aid, rich in possibilities, which will take into account any number of variables. This topic will be discussed in depth in the chapter on *Nomographic Calculation*.

4: General Classification of All Methods of Mechanical and Graphical Calculation

A collection of all the methods for calculation, both geometrical and mechanical, would at first sight appear to form a very large and confused mass. The deep study of these methods, in which we have been engaged for over thirty years, has led us finally to use two characteristics for each method: first, the method by which the numbers involved in the calculation (the data and the results) are given to or obtained from the device; and second, the nature (graphical or mechanical) of the relation by means of which the operation is performed.

Consider first the question of how the numbers are supplied or obtained. Either the digits comprising each number are written individually by some suitable device, the number of digits in each case being limited by practical considerations, in which case we have a *digital system*; or each number is read on a graduated scale (linear or functional), which forms an *analogue system*. The second method is practical only to a certain degree of approximation because, unless a number is the same as one of those used for graduating the scale, interpolation between marked points has to be done by eye. In using the analogue system, the degree of approximation must be adequate for the intended application.

It is the relation between the digital and analogue systems that constitutes the very essence of the process in question. This fundamental consideration leads to a grouping of the processes into five classes, which, with their subdivisions, form the framework of the present volume.

Among these five classes only one is based on the use of *digital input and output*. This includes all those devices that may be properly called calculating machines. Such machines are used only for separate arithmetical operations or combinations of small numbers of operations, such as the tiers of additions on which the calculus of differences depends. They may work with numbers of as many digits as necessary, within the limits of practical consideration. It is convenient to restrict the name *Mechanical Calculation* to this class of machines.

The remaining four classes of devices use only analogue scales. In the first instance, scales can be used simply to give the lengths of segments of lines on a drawing, which can be proportional either to the input or output numbers themselves, which is the usual case, or to some simple function of these numbers, such as the square or the logarithm. These line segments, representing the data, are then used in geometrical constructions that have been designed so that the required computational result appears also as a line segment and its value can be read on a graduated scale. These constructions can be made either by ordinary graphical methods involving the use of only ruler, set-square, and compass, or by mechanical devices whose operations express certain geometrical relations. Examples of the latter include the various integrometers and integraphs. In the first case, that of purely graphical construction, we are dealing with what is properly called *Graphical Calculation*, which includes the whole of *Graphical Statics*; in the second, with *Grapho-Mechanical Calculation*.

We may also suppose, however, that graduated scales are used directly in operations that replace numerical calculation. In this case the various scales must be linked together by certain systems of lines, which can be either fixed or movable, or by certain mechanical devices, in such a way that if, at any instant, numbers are read on all the scales simultaneously against some previously determined indexes, a certain analytic relation holds among these numbers. A representation has thus been found for this relation. Depending on the linking between the different scales being either graphical or mechanical, it gives rise to two new classes, *Nomographic Calculation* and *Nomo-Mechanical Calculation*, respectively.

The scales used in nomograms are not only those we have called by the special name of *analogue systems*. In fact graduated lines of any type may also be used. In order to conform to the fundamental type defined here, it is sufficient to note that any graduated line can be represented as a series of functional lines on which the graduated points are noted as the intersections with a series of transversal lines.[40]

So far as nomo-mechanical calculation is concerned, this term includes not only devices such as calculating rules and circles, but also the remarkable machines, which he termed *algebraic*, invented by Torres Quevedo.

To summarize, the classification of all geometrical and mechanical methods of calculation can be reduced to the following table:

1. Mechanical Calculation
2. Graphical Calculation
3. Grapho-Mechanical Calculation
4. Nomographic Calculation
5. Nomo-Mechanical Calculation

A chapter is devoted to each of these special types of calculation in the rest of this work. We must remark, however, that some of these are not always separated by clearcut boundaries. In particular, if a nomogram, which in principle belongs to the fourth class, has been constructed with some physical device to bring about those contacts on which its operation depends, it can be assigned to the fifth class. Thus we have put in this class, for example, logarithmic instruments, which could equally be regarded as nomograms with movable scales.

Notes

1. *Notions sur la Machine Analytique de Ch. Babbage* (*Bibliothèque Universelle de Genève*, Vol. XLI, p. 352).

2. From the following sources: *Biographie de Henri Mondeux* (6th edition) by Émile Jacoby, Mondeux's teacher; an article by A. Béligne in *Revue Encyclopédique* (1892, p. 1295); *Psychologie des Grands Calculateurs et Joueurs d'Échecs*, by Alfred Binet (Hachette, 1894), who refers also to a memoir by Mr. Scripture in the *American Journal of Psychology* (Vol. IV, April 1881, p. 1). Other works that may be consulted are the report on Mondeux by Cauchy (*C.R.*, 2nd session 1840, p. 952) and on Inaudi by Charcot and Darboux (*C.R.*, 1st session 1892, p. 1329).

3. *Mémoires*, Vol. VIII, p. 105. In Jacoby's work Mme. de Lingré's name is given as Luatré.

4. These first names of Buxton and Colburn are given by Béligne; Jacoby gives Judéiah and Zerald, respectively.

5. Given by Bobynin in an article in *Enseignement Mathématique* (1904, p. 362) in which he makes the same distinction as that given here between calculators and mathematicians. He misspells most of the names—e.g., Mondé for Mondeux, Kolborn for Colbourn.

6. As a result of some confusion, Binet, in his book (p. 189) erroneously attributes this disability to Prolongeau (see *C.R.* Vol. XXXIV, 1852, p. 371).

7. According to an article by H. Laurent on *Calcul Mental* in the *Grande Encyclopédie du XIXe Siècle*.

8. Binet's book gives reports of some very detailed studies made on the calculating prodigies Inaudi and Diamandi, attributing an aural memory to the first and a visual memory to the second:

> In the course of a private session on 6 June 1924, which was conducted in a rigorously scientific manner, Inaudi willingly submitted himself to a comparative test with some of the machines to be described later in this book. While his speed of mental calculation is astonishing and puts him in the first rank of calculating prodigies, it has to be stated that the machines soon begin to overtake him as the number of figures involved in the calculations increases. For example, in multiplications the machines' advantage begins to show at the level of 4 figures times 4 figures and increases rapidly from there on. This is not surprising in view of the fact that some of these machines, admittedly when worked by particularly skillful and well-trained operators, can give an 8 figure by 8 figure product in under 6 seconds.

9. *Rev. de la R. Ac. de Cienc.* Vol. XXIII, Num. 2, Dec. 1926, p. 313.

10. This misconception permeates the whole of the book on Mondeux by his teacher Jacoby, who nevertheless reports a number of facts that are sufficient to contradict it. For example: "... He either could not, or would not, listen to a single word of theory and I was never able to get him to give a proof..." (p. 128); "... In spite of all my teaching and my efforts Henri barely knew, indeed I can go so far as to say that he did not know, the first four books of Legendre's *Géométrie*..." (p. 131); "... I was never able to get Mondeux to make any study of the science he loved so much, or to explain his methods of calculation."

The view we have given is confirmed further by what Jacoby reports in other part of his book (pp. 9, 10, 11) concerning the failure of his attempts to impart mathematical education to other calculating prodigies (Dinner, Collburn, Mangiamelle).

One of the strangest features reported by Jacoby is that Mondeux was already in possession of all his calculating powers long before he had been taught the forms of the figures. To us, who can only work with numbers in terms of their representation by figures, there is something incomprehensible here.

11. ***6*** p. 214 (Ed.) References of this type refer to items cited in the bibliography at the end of this volume.

12. Whose name, Latinized to Neperus, became Neper in French.

13. (Ed.) Interested readers are refered to: Williams, M. R. "From Napier to Lucas: The Use of Napier's Bones in Calculating Instruments," *Annals of the History of Computing*, Vol. 5, Num. 3, July 1983, pp. 279–296.

14. (Ed.) This illustration was not in the original French edition, but has been added by the editors.

15. *Journal des Savants*, 1678, p. 162.

16. *C.R.*, 28 October, 1839.

17. *Journal des Savants*, 1678, p. 162

18. *Theatrum Arithmetico-Geometricum*, p. 25.

19. *Arithmétique Allemande*, p. 495.

20. *Mém. de l'Acad. des Sciences*, 1740, Vol. V.

21. *Hist. de l'Acad.* des Sciences, 1740, p. 59.

22. *C.R.*, 7 October, 1867.

23. *Illustration*, July 1911.

24. *La Nature*, July 1920 and October 1925.

25. The list of references given with the paper by Th. Olivier (*B.S.E.* 1843, p. 415), from which we have taken much of this information, includes also two machines due to Mr. Nuisement (1834), which would seem to be more properly put into our fourth class.

26. Referred to by Ed. Lucas in his *Théorie des Nombres* (p. 32). There are some sets in the Conservatoire des Arts et Métiers.

27. (Ed.) This paragraph actually appeared as an extra note printed on a separate page, bound just before page 1, in the original volume. The editors though it best to put it in context.

28. This device was given the name *Prompt Multiplicateur et Diviseur*. On May 27 of the same year, 1841, J. S. Henri took out a patent for what he called the *Prompt Calculateur*, to which Eggis's *auto multiplicateur* (see ***6***, p. 235) could be attached. The principle on which these various multipliers are based had been used by Petit in 1671.

29. Genaille, who died on 16 May 1903, had a veritable genius for the invention of arithmetical instruments. Among the unusual devices he produced we may mention a ruler equipped with pegs with which the primality of numbers of the form $2^n - 1$ can be tested; with this he was able to verify that certain very large numbers of this form, given by Fermat, are prime—although no one knows how the great mathematician arrived at this result. Genaille had also drafted a design for an electrical calculating machine but, unfortunately, this was never constructed. See also *A.F.A.S.*, Congrès de Marseille, 1891, p. 159.

30. In a note in *Journal de Crelle* (Vol. 28, 1844, p. 184) a Russian inventor named Slonimsky extols the advantages of an apparatus that he does not describe but that, from what the writes, must give results in a way similar to Genaille's rulers. A method of the same type was proposed by Jofe in 1841 (see ***14***, p. 194).

31. At first sight this number certainly seems very great; but to give a better idea of how very great it is we shall use a striking comparison due to Édouard Lucas:

> Suppose we wish to print all the results that can be given by this device. If we arrange for the 9 products corresponding to each number to be printed on a single line we shall need one hundred quintillion lines. If the lines are spaced 1 centimeter apart this will require a strip of paper whose length is 25,000,000,000 times the circumference of the earth, which means that if this were to be wrapped around the earth by the daily rotation process it would take more than 68 million years.
>
> Suppose now that this catalogue of results was formed into pages of 100 lines each, bound into volumes of 1000 pages: it would comprise 1,000,000,000,000 (*one quadrillion*) Volumes! Given that the Bibilothèque Nationale could hold 10 million volumes of this large size (which is a reasonable estimate), then a building one hundred million times the size of the Bibliothèque Nationale would be needed to hold the catalogue! Such numbers, whose size defies the imagination, serve to show the extraordinary calculating powers of this little apparatus whose perimeter is only a few decimeters long.

32. All these rulers were sold in Paris by the E. Bellin company. Édouard Lucas designed a perpetual calendar based on a similar principle to that of Genaille's rulers. It consists of a set of rulers carrying only the black pointers and corresponding, respectively, to the century, the year within the century, the month, the date within the month, and finally the day of the week. When the rulers are arranged appropriately the black pointers form a broken line, at the end of which the required result is read. This calender is shown in the 4 January 1890 issue of *Revue Scientifique*. Also similar to Genaille's rulers is the device know as the Espéranto of L. Cabrol (1907).

33. (Ed.) Often called *difference methods*.

34. See the later section on Difference Machines in Chapter I. This method for constructing tables can be extended to more complicated functions if, as a result of a mathematical analysis, they are replaced, to the required degree of approximation and over a stated interval, by polynomials constituting the significant terms of the developments in power series.

35. (Ed.) The "official" translation of *barème* is "ready-reckoner"; it seemed better to keep the French.

36. Since that time, tables of this type have been produced in such quantity to meet the needs of commerce and finance that there can be no question of giving even an incomplete listing.

37. It may be convenient to reduce the bulk of a single-entry table by transforming it into a double-entry table, taking as arguments the tens and units digits, respectively. This is done, in particular, in the case of tables of logarithms.

38. Made up of Mrs. Cayley, Stokes, W. Thomson, Smith, and Glaisher.

39. (Ed.) It is worth remarking that this is analagous to the modification of Napier's bones produced by Schott, as described earlier.

40. In connection with these methods for calculating it can be stated that any mathematical law ('nomos' in Greek) can be expressed either graphically or mechanically.

Chapter I: Mechanical Calculation

1.1: Arithmetical Instruments

We shall give the name *arithmetical instruments* to those devices that enable the arithmetical operations to be performed manually without the aid of any mechanism in the strict sense of the term, that is, without the use of cams, springs, gears, etc. These instruments have been produced by people in all nations from their earliest times. We must include with them the ancient *Roman abacus*[1] and the various types of bead frame, used very widely in Europe throughout the Middle Ages and still in use today in several forms such as the Russian *Stchoty*, the Chinese *Swan-pan*,[2] and the Japanese *Soroban*.[3]

The principle on which instruments for performing addition are based is as follows: Suppose we have a graduated ruler that can be moved with respect to a fixed index; if we move this first by n' divisions with respect to the index, then by n'', then by n''', etc., the total number of divisions that have crossed the index will be the sum $n' + n'' + n''' + \cdots$.[4]

We can apply this principle by taking as the index the zero mark on a fixed ruler that has the same graduations as a movable ruler and sliding the latter along the former, at each step bringing to the index the division on the movable ruler that is opposite the mark on the fixed ruler corresponding to the next number to be added. *Figure 4* shows the successive positions of the movable ruler m with respect to the fixed ruler f in the addition $3 + 6$.

This very simple principle can be applied equally to the case of a circular disk that can be turned inside a circle, the two being graduated in the same way as the two rulers.[5] The principle can also be applied to an arrangement in which a ring slides around the periphery of a disk, as was done in the instruments made by Lagrous[6] (1828) and by Briet[7] (1829).

Using the method just described for large numbers would require rulers of inconvenient size; but we can limit the rulers to ten divisions marked 0 to 9, place several sets side by side, and assign one set to the units, one to the tens, one to the hundreds, and so on. Such an arrangement can be seen in an instrument built by an inventor called de Caze[8] in 1720 and now in the Conservatoire des Arts et Métiers. This instrument is interesting in that, even at this date, it uses complement subtraction. A difficulty that arises with this scheme is that of passing the carries from one column to the next, but, as a consequence of a clever observation, this can be done without any need to complicate the instrument.[9] This observation was used in Kummer's instrument[10] in 1847, and is still applied in Troncet's *arith-*

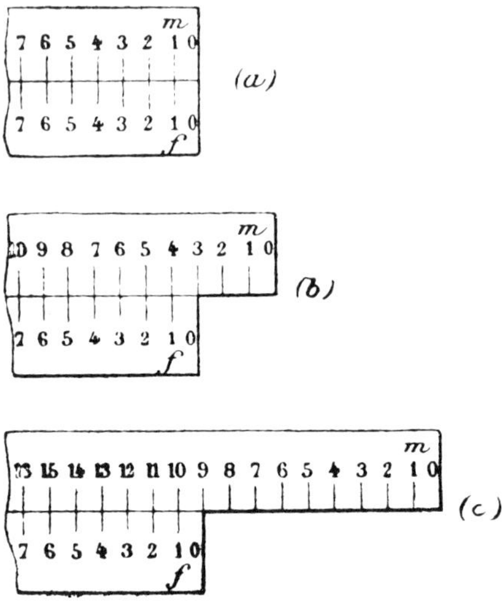

Figure 4

mographe (similar to that shown in *Figure 5*) in the following form:

> To enter a digit into one of the columns, the point of the stylus is inserted into the hole adjacent to the required digit marked on the edge of the slot. This hole is formed by the space between the teeth of a rack: if these teeth are white, the stylus is moved down the slot until it meets the stop at the bottom; if they are black or red, it is moved upward and to the end of the curved part at the top, forming a crook.

With Troncet's instrument all that has to be done is to enter the numbers to be added, using the first column on the right for the units, the next for the tens, the third for the hundreds, and so on; the total appears in the windows at the bottom. Subtraction is done in the same way, the larger number being first put in the upper windows where the result is seen.

Many variations on this type of adder have been produced in recent years: *Addiator*, *Robo*, *Procalculo*, *Francia*, *Picma* (for English currency); *Hora* (for hours, minutes, seconds, and fifths);[11] etc. L. Cabrol's *arithmographe*, which used curved slots, was also based on the same principle.[12] In other variants due to Diakoff[13] and Webb[14] (*Ribbon Adders*[15]) the racks are replaced by ribbons wrapped around cylinders.

A fast method for multiplication can be obtained by combining the use of an adder of the type just described with that of a compact form of the multiplication table such as that due to Napier or Genaille described

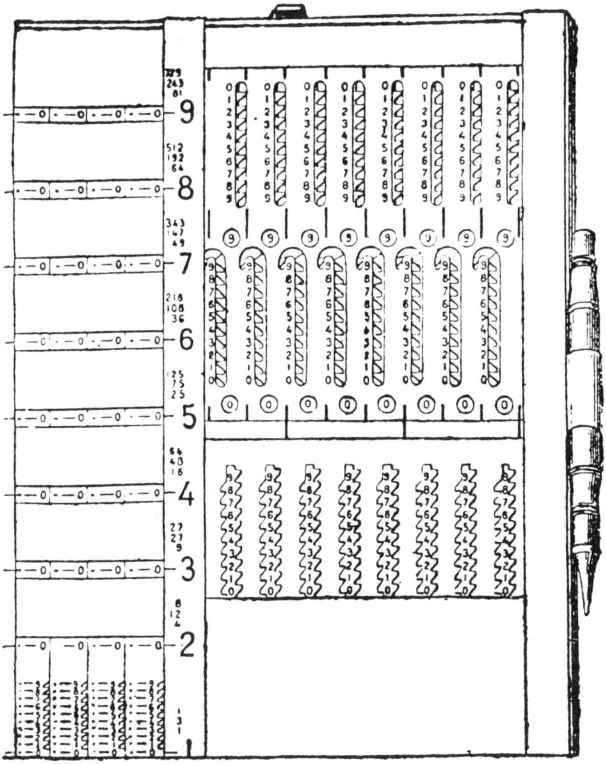

Figure 5

earlier. Other instruments have been designed with the aim of providing the partial products, ready for addition: an example is the *multiplier-divisor table* due to Léon Bollée.[16] Bollées device is a modification of Napier's bones[17] in which two sets of movable rulers are placed, one on top of the other, at right angles. If one factor of a multiplication is placed on the horizontal rulers and the second on the verticals, the product is found by simply adding up the digits seen, on the diagonal, through small windows in the top set of rulers. It has been estimated that this increases the speed of multiplication by three times over the ordinary method.

Another method is first to form the partial products by means of a multiplication table and then to use an adder to find their sum. In the apparatus due to Michel Rous[18] (1869) these are given by cylinders similar to Schott's, the reading of which is aided by their having bands of different colors, and the sum found with the aid of a bead frame or by means of numbered disks. Esersky[19] (1872) also based his instrument on the use of a bead frame. In other instruments the multiplication table is joined to an adder of the slotted type, as in the final model of Troncet's arithmographe[20] (*Figure 5*). An instrument in the same class, in which the adder is joined to the multiplier, was devised by Pope,[21] however, the detailed arrangement is quite different from that used by Rous and Esersky, the latter two being virtually identical to each other.

The question arises, however, of the possibility of totaling the partial products automatically as they are formed, without the need to copy them to another device. Once again the problem has been solved by Genaille in a device displayed in the Conservatoire des Arts et Métiers. This instrument consists of a set of rulers that can be moved lengthwise, each of which carries a special scale, which we may call a *sliding scale*, and an index mark on its lower end. The other markings resemble those found on a standard set of Genaille rulers.

In determining the product of two numbers, the rulers are selected to represent the multiplicand and, as in the ordinary use of Genaille rulers, the product digits are read off from the line corresponding to the units digit of the multiplier. As each of the digits is read, by following the left pointing triangles, the ruler is moved so that its index coincides with the mark on the sliding scale of the preceding ruler corresponding to this digit. With this new setting of the rulers, the process is repeated for the tens figure of the multiplier, and so on. At each step, the first digit on the right of the result gives a digit of the final product. When using the highest order digit of the multiplier the rulers are not moved and the last digits of the product are simply read out in the usual way.

After a little practice the operation can be performed very quickly. Genaille has made it even easier by replacing the successive longitudinal positions taken by the rulers with a set of overlapping plates. These plates are numbered so as to eliminate the need for sliding one ruler against the others.

Independently of Genaille, Léon Bollée, whose fine multiplying machine will be described later, has made an instrument for directly finding the product of pairs of numbers, each of several digits.[22] This consists of a set of rulers, similar to Genaille's and equipped with overlapping plates

Figure 6

mounted on a movable carriage, each of which may be turned over to expose a different digit, together with an adding mechanism of the type found in the Troncet arithmometer, but without the colors on the toothed racks. There now being no indication of the direction in which the stylus is to be moved, it is *always* moved upward as though to be taken to the curved portion of the slot; however, if it meets a stop before reaching the end, it is then taken back to the bottom. All the fundamental arithmetical operations can be performed with this instrument, including the extraction of square roots. With the model shown in *Figure 6* a product with up to 14 digits can be obtained when multipliers of a maximum of 6 digits are used.

It is very simple to operate this instrument. The multiplier is set on the numbered plates, by exposing those whose numbers in succession form the digits of the multiplier; the adding mechanism is then used as described above, using each digit of the multiplicand in turn, and shifting the movable part of the mechanism one place to the left after processing each digit.

It is clear that the number of movements increases with the number of digits that have to be used. Some further mechanism must be introduced if any great speed is to be attained, and it is this that gives the advantage to the machines we shall now describe.

1.2: Arithmetical Machines

1.2.1: Machines for Simple Operations

1.2.1.1: General Description of Arithmetical Machines

In the interests of clarity of the explanations to follow, we start with a general outline of the properties of arithmetical machines.[23]

The essential component of all machines of this type is what we shall call the *figure wheel.* This is a circular cylinder that can rotate about its axis and has the digits 0 to 9 inscribed at regular intervals around a circle either on one of the ends or on the curved surface. Above the *figure wheel* is a fixed plate with a window through which one digit at a time can be seen as the cylinder turns. In some cases the 0–9 numbering is repeated several times around the circle.

If initially the digit n is seen in the window and the cylinder is then turned through 1, 2, 3, . . . fractions of a complete revolution that correspond to the movement from one digit to the next (we shall simply say by 1, 2, 3, etc., *units*), in the direction opposite to that of the numbering, the figure seen through the window will be the units digit of $n + 1$, $n + 2$, $n + 3$, etc.

Suppose several such figure wheels are placed side by side so that the digits seen in the respective windows, taken together, represent a number in the decimal scale. This system forms a *counter*. If the figures seen in the windows corresponding to the units, tens, hundreds, etc., are $a_0, a_1, a_2, \ldots,$ a_p, respectively, the number represented is $a_p \ldots a_2 a_1 a_0$.

If the wheels are turned by b_0, b_1, b_2, . . . , b_p units, respectively, the figures seen in the windows will be the digits of the sum of $a_p \ldots a_2 a_1 a_0$ and $b_p \ldots b_2 b_1 b_0$ *apart from the carries.* To take these into account, as it moves from position 9 to position 0 during this operation, it must cause the figure wheel of the next higher decimal order to advance by one unit.

There are two main possibilities for the arrangement of the figure wheels. In one they turn about parallel axes arranged either in one plane or around one circular cylinder, and in the other they all turn about the same axis. In the first case the numbers are said to be *multiaxial*, either *linear* or *circular*, and the numbering can be either on the flat sides or on the curved surfaces of the cylinders, but in either case they are written on a line perpendicular to the axis of the cylinder. In the second case the counter is said to be *uniaxial*, the figures necessarily on the curved surfaces and written on lines *parallel to*

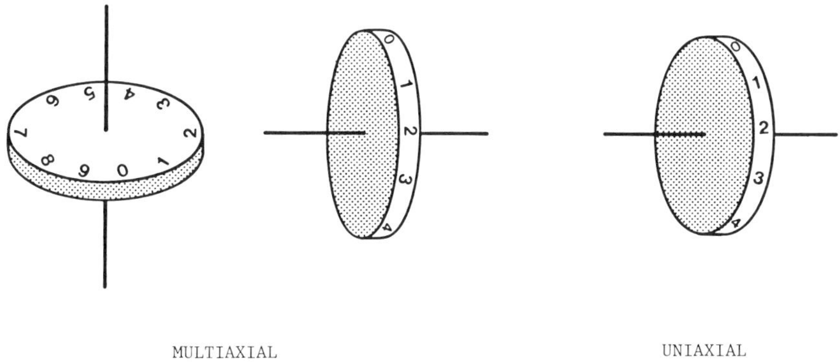

Figure 6a

the axis. The two cases are most easily distinguished by an inspection of *Figure 6a*.[24]

If this device is to constitute a machine in the proper sense of the word, it must be provided with some means for making the carries automatically, without any need for attention on the part of the operator; the means for doing this, which must be repeated between each pair of consecutive figure wheels, is called the *carry mechanism*. A counter does not constitute a machine unless it is equipped with such a mechanism.

Some special means must be provided to turn each figure wheel through exactly the number of units intended; we shall call this the *driver* for the wheel. It may be possible for each driver to move its wheel individually, and this is in fact what is done in certain machines, particularly the old adding machines; but a mechanism can be imagined that, when all the drivers have been set so as to give each figure wheel the rotation appropriate to the number it is to register, moves them all simultaneously: this device will be called the *setting mechanism*.

Finally, if it is wished to be able to automatically return all the figure wheels to zero after each operation, there must be a special mechanism for this, the *zeroizer* or *clearing mechanism*.

1.2.1.2: Application to the Different Arithmetical Operations

So far we have discussed only additions, either individual ($a + b = c$) or cumulative ($a + b + c + \cdots + k = l$). If subtraction has to be done, either individual ($a - b = c$) or successive ($a - b - c - \cdots - k = l$), everything that has been said already remains valid, with the only difference that now the figure wheel must be turned in the same direction as the numbering instead of in the opposite direction as before.

To achieve this with the machine already described, either the direction of numbering the figure wheels must be changed, but the direction of rotation kept as before, or vice versa. If the first choice is made, it will suffice to add a second numbering to each wheel, going in the direction opposite to the first, and visible through a second window—with the arrangement that only one set of windows, corresponding to addition or to subtraction, is open at any one time. With the second choice it must be made possible to reverse the direction of rotation of the wheels without impeding the action of the carry mechanism. According to the choice made we say that the wheels are, or are not, *reversible*.

The first choice, providing different numberings for addition and subtraction, would seem unsuitable when subtractions have to be combined with additions ($a + b + c - d - \cdots + k = l$), as is often the case, and therefore it would seem at first sight that subtraction should be done only with machines having reversible wheels. However, a very simple trick makes it possible to use nonreversible wheels, with only a single numbering, for this purpose, so that, although machines are no longer made with separate numberings for addition and subtraction, it can be said that any machine that can add can also subtract.

The trick is to use complements: if the machine uses n digits, add the complement with respect to 10^n of the number to be subtracted. The result sought ($a - b$) and the result found ($a + (10^n - b)$) differ only by 10^n, that is, by 1 in the $(n + 1)$th place, which does not appear since the machine works to only n digits.

The number $10^n - b$ can be formed by taking the complement with respect to 9 of each digit of the number to be subtracted, except for the least significant digit, for which the complement with respect to 10 is taken. As the number to be subtracted will usually have fewer than n digits, its complement will have as many 9s on the left as it would need 0s to make up a number of n digits. If one or more of these 9s are omitted, which is equivalent to taking the complement with respect to, say, 10^{n-1} or 10^{n-2}, a unit will appear in the position corresponding to the order $n - 1$ or $n - 2$. This property is used to give the quotient[25] when dividing, with a machine on which subtraction is done by addition of the complement, because 1 is added to the position on the left of the last 9 for every subtraction made, thus effectively counting the number of subtractions.

Multiplication can be done by repeated addition, and division by subtraction repeated until the remainder is less than the divisor. It need scarcely be said that these repetitions are not made one by one in numbers equal to the size of the multiplier or of the dividend, but rather in the successive decimal positions, the number at each step being given by the corresponding digit of the multiplier or quotient.

It seems evident that the use of a setting mechanism will greatly simplify the operation when these repetitions are concerned, because at each decimal position of the figure wheels all the drivers, in whatever number are needed, must be made to act. However, we shall see later that in certain conditions this greater simplicity is not necessarily accompanied by greater speed.

Having set out these definitions, we are now in a position to give, in a few words, an adequately detailed description of the various types of arithmetical machine, restricting ourselves in each case to a few characteristic models.

1.2.2: Machines without Setting Mechanisms

1.2.2.1: Multiaxial Counter with Simple Drivers

This is the type of the first[26] calculating machine to be built, that of Blaise Pascal, the invention of which goes back to 1642[27] (calculating instruments, having no mechanisms in the strict sense of the word, are not counted here). *Figure 7* shows the exterior appearance of this machine, and *Figure 8* a plan view of its mechanical components.

The driver for each figure wheel is formed by the movable spokes of a wheel whose fixed rim is numbered from 0 to 9 and has a peg between the 0 and the 9 (*Figure 9*). A stylus, called by Pascal the *directeur*, is inserted into the opening corresponding to one of the digits marked on the rim and the neighboring spoke pushed clockwise to the peg. This action turns all the spokes, and consequently the figure wheel fixed to the same axis,[28] by a number of units equal to the original digit.

The crucial feature of Pascal's invention is the carry mechanism, and it is this that gives it the property of a true machine.

As this book is not addressed to specialists in mechanical engineering, we shall give only a broad indication of the working of this mechanism, which Pascal called the *sautoir*. Just before the origin of the numbering on a wheel (the point separating 9 and 0) passes the peg, the movement of the wheel

Figure 7

Figure 8

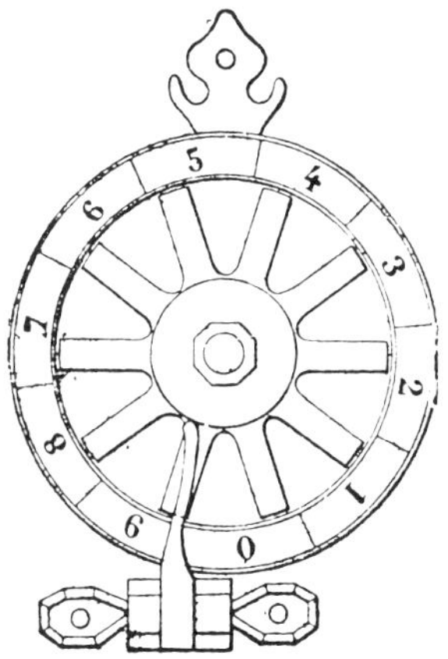

Figure 9

starts a weight to turn in an upward direction about a horizontal axis.[29] A suitably placed catch releases the weight at the exact moment of passing the peg, and in falling back to its original position it causes the next wheel on the left to advance one unit. Such a mechanism can work for only one direction of rotation of the wheels, so Pascal's machine is not reversible. It has a single set of windows, of which one-half show the result of addition and the other subtraction; a sliding screen allows only one or the other to be visible at any one time. This screen can be seen at the top of *Figure 7*, where the addition windows are open.

These arrangements, with which Pascal remained content, were modified by several workers, including Lépine[30] (1725) and Hillerin de Boistissandeau[31] (1730). Other developments that diverged more from Pascal's ideas, but remained based on the same principles, were made by Sir Samuel Morland[32] (1663), the Marquis Poleni[33] (1709), and Gersten[34] (1735). It was not until 1841 that Pascal's original ideas were given a really satisfactory practical realization in the adding machine due to Dr. Roth.[35] In this the digits were written around the edges of simple disks, an arrangement that enabled the dimensions of the machine to be reduced significantly. From the mechanical point of view the most significant improvement was that the energy for driving the carry mechanism was provided by a spring that was wound up by the movement of the figure wheel as it turned from 0 to 9 and was realized at the instant of passing from 9 to 0.

Because the energy accumulates regularly during the rotation of the figure wheel from 0 to 9 (approximately 1/9 of the total energy required is added at the passage of each figure) the carry mechanism works with great regularity in comparison with Pascal's *sautoir*, which is raised during less than half a rotation. This valuable feature of Roth's adder enabled the inventor to base his zeroing process on the smooth working of the carry mechanism. A knob on the side of the machine, when pulled, causes a rack to move, and this, in turn, will rotate each of the figure wheels to the point where they are each showing a 9 in their windows; it then automatically adds 1 in the first position on the right, resulting in all the 9s being replaced by 0s.

Among modern machines that are descendants of Pascal's are the *Samostchoty* of Bouniaskovsky[36] (1867), the two circle adder of C. H. Webb[37] (1868), the adder with rack mechanism of Leiner[38] (1878), and finally the machine due to G. Orlin[39](1892), the workings of which depend on the engagement of threaded rods with nuts, the latter capable of being moved longitudinally without rotation.

The *Addermaschine* of Baum and the *Conto* of Aumund can be considered to be machines in the same class as Roth's.

1.2.2.2: Uniaxial Counter with Simple Drivers

It is clear that the use of a uniaxial counter would have the advantage of reducing the amount of machinery required. The first such use was in 1750 in the machine built by J. I. Pereire.[40] In this machine the figure wheels took the form of disks, numbered around their rims, all mounted on the same axis. In addition to the digits, each disk had a series of holes, which could be seen through a slot in the machine's cover. The edges of each slot were also numbered so that a needle inserted in one of the holes enabled the disk to be turned any desired number of digits.

A machine of this same type was proposed a few years ago[41] by an Italian engineer, Mr. Fossa-Mancini; this device is a very nice combination of mechanical devices and, in particular, has an ingenious system for counterbalancing the inertial forces brought into play when the machine is operated at great speed. However, for a particularly original type of uniaxial counter, we must look at Tchebichef's, shown later in this volume as *Figures 63–66* in Appendix I. In this machine the figure wheels are drums mounted on a single axis and having the numbers 0 to 9 repeated three times around their peripheries; each is turned by a driving wheel, mounted on the same axis, which itself can be turned by means of pins fixed in its rim. The pins correspond in position to the digits 1, 2, . . . , 9, which are marked on the cylindrical cover of the machine. The characteristic feature of this machine is that the carry process works continuously, each stage consisting of an epicyclic train of ratio 10 (visible in some of the spaces between consecutive drums in *Figure 63*, which shows the machine without its cover).

Such an arrangement can work whatever the direction of rotation, so that Tchebichef's machine, in contrast to all those discussed so far, is reversible. However, since the carries change the positions of the successive figures only gradually, these positions will differ from those produced in a machine having a discontinuous carry mechanism; but since the angular difference between the two positions is always less than that corresponding to one unit, reading can be made possible by providing windows of sufficient width for two consecutive digits to be seen simultaneously. The choice of which digit is to be taken when reading the result is guided by bands marked in white on the periphery of each drum (see *Figure 63*) that take into account the angular displacement of the following drum.[42]

An epicyclic gear train is also used in the Burroughs Calculator, but here the transfer is completed by a second such train, called the "reading correction." This second train, with the aid of a cam, replaces the continuous advance of the figure wheel by a stationary period while the preceding wheel is turning from 0 to 9, followed by the complete transfer, resulting in a movement of 1/10 of a turn, as that wheel moves from 9 to 0. Thus all the figures of the result are always exactly in a straight line, as was the case in the earlier machines, but this arrangement removes the advantage of reversibility from the counter.

1.2.2.3: Key-Operated Drivers

In all the counters described so far the drivers are what we have called simple; that is, the operator gives the required rotation to each figure wheel by hand, the extent of his movement being determined by the particular numbering and limited simply by a stop. One can see, however, that this rotation could be communicated to the figure wheels by some mechanism driven by keys corresponding to the digits to be entered. On first consideration one might be tempted to see this only as an unnecessary complication, but the great advantage from the point of view of using the machine soon becomes apparent. With the simple driver the whole hand has to be used in moving each individual wheel, but with this new arrangement only a single finger need be applied to a key.

This idea seems to have been put into practice for the first time in a machine built by V. Schilt[43] and displayed at the Great Exhibition of 1851 in London. It appeared again in connection with the addition of numbers consisting of a single-digit in machines due to F. Arzberger[44] (1866), Stettner[45] (1882), Bagge[46] (1884), d'Azevedo (1884), Pététin[47] (1885), Max Mayer[48](1886), and Shohé Tanaka[49] (1893). In 1873 Bieringer and Hebetanz[50] built a machine having keys and a clockwork movement.

It was, however, in America that key-driven machines were given the really practical form that enabled them to become industrial products. These machines have a number of columns of keys, the keys in each column being numbered from 1 to 9. Pressing any of these keys results in the number engraved on it being entered into that column. When a complete number has been entered in this way all that is necessary is to pull a lever for that number to be added to the total already formed and to be printed on a strip of paper that issues from a roll held in the back of the machine. Machines of this type are the Felt and Tarrant *comptometer*[51] (1887)[52] (*Figure 10*), the *Burroughs Calculator* (1888), and the Heinitz[53] machine. In Bahmann's machine[54] (1888) the total is not printed but is shown by the position of a pointer, as in a meter.

Figure 10

These machines may have either a single set of keys, which act on each of the figure wheels in succession, or one set for every decimal position, thus allowing several figure wheels to be acted on simultaneously if necessary. The two different configurations are called "reduced (10-key) keyboard" or "full keyboard," respectively.

The reduced keyboard is found mainly in machines that are typewriters with attached adders, such as the Remington-Wahl, Smith-Premier-Accounting, Elliott-Fisher, etc. These have, in addition to the usual ten keys numbered 0 to 9, a toothed wheel that plays the part of the driver. As each key is pressed it turns the wheel by a number of teeth equal to the number on that key. The adder is usually of a special type called a "cross," and can either add or subtract according to the direction in which it is driven; it is reset to zero by subtracting its current contents.

Intermediate between the reduced and the full keyboard machines is Runge's machine[55] (1896). This had only two sets of keys and a device that enables any digit to be entered into any decimal position. One set of keys is used to determine the digit, and the other the position into which it is to be entered.

The advantage of a full keyboard machine over the old style stylus set machines (of which Tchebichef's was the last to be developed) is not only that they replace the stylus by keys, but also that any number fewer than ten digits (and it is rare in practice that so many are needed) can be entered with one stroke of the fingers, as though striking a chord on the piano: in the language of piano playing, we may say that the number is *struck* on the machine. The gain in time resulting from using the keys is very evident when the sum of a long series of numbers has to be found. The method of "striking" the keys can also be used to perform multiplication: the multiplicand is struck first in the units position a number of times equal to the units digit of the multiplier, then in the tens position a number of times equal to the tens digit, etc. The manual skill of the operators is clearly important here. They must be trained to play on the keyboard in the style of a pianist. This facility is also necessary with the calculating typewriter described above.

Experience has shown that an operator of these machines, after sufficient training to have mastered the technique, can perform multiplications more quickly than is possible with the machines having setting mechanisms, which will be described later.[56] The machines with setting mechanisms, however, have the advantage that the amount of teaching required in order to make use of them is reduced to a minimum. They also provide some protection from "false notes," which can escape from a too impetuous operator of a key-driven machine.

We remarked earlier that the numbers being entered into an addition were, so to speak, "struck" on the keyboard. In practice, this only applies strictly to multiplication, for which the possibility of there being such a method of operation is an essential requirement. Numbers will be entered this way during the early stages of learning, but an operator will soon master a different technique, called "the method of touch": here only the keys 1 to 5 are used, the number 6 being entered by striking 3 twice, 7 by striking 4 and 3 in succession, and so on. The tops of the even keys differ from those of the odd, and this, together with the small spread of the fingers needed to reach all the keys in this smaller set, makes it possible to keep the hand in one position and to work without looking at the keyboard. As in piano playing, the eyes are kept on the document and do not have to be moved to the keys, a practice that is both tiring and prejudicial to performance.

The construction of the driving mechanism for key-operated machines can be explained in outline as follows. Each column of keys is at the right of the corresponding figure wheel. Striking a key causes pressure to be exerted on a lever at a particular point, and this lever has at its end a toothed sector that engages with a gear fixed rigidly to the figure wheel. According to the position at which this pressure is applied the sector moves 1, 2, . . . , 9 teeth and so turns the figure wheel through that number of units. This, more or less, is the arrangement in the Felt and Tarrant *Comptometer*[57] and in the *Burroughs Calculator*. The above description can best be appreciated by a careful examination of *Figure 10a*.[58]

These machines have a zeroizer operated with a single movement of a lever. Originally this acted in the same way as that in Roth's adder, first causing all the figure wheels to rotate in their normal direction until they all registered a 9, and then adding 1 to the rightmost digit. The current arrangement is that the figure wheels are all returned to zero directly by rotating them in the opposite direction.

No special mechanisms are provided for subtraction; instead, each key top has, in small characters, the complement of the number that would be used for addition. This makes the use of complement methods, as described earlier, significantly easier.

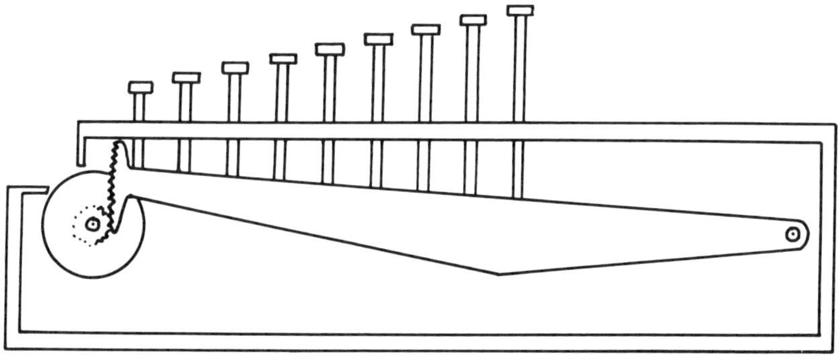

Figure 10a

1.2.3: Machines with Setting Mechanisms

1.2.3.1: Gears with Teeth of Unequal Length

We have already mentioned the advantage to be gained, during the operations of multiplication and division, from providing the machine with a means of rotating all the figure wheels *simultaneously*.

The earliest proposal for a means of doing this is the one put forward by Leibniz in 1671. In this scheme the rotation of each figure wheel is determined by having a gear, fixed to the figure wheel axis, engage with a drum gear having nine teeth of integer lengths, the lengths increasing in an arithmetic progression. The gear fixed to the wheel axis can be made to engage the drum gear at places where there are one, two, . . . , or nine teeth. A lay shaft, driven by a handle, communicates its rotation to all the drum gears simultaneously, each making a complete turn. The situation can be easily seen illustrated in *Figure 11a.*[59]

It is worth repeating that Leibniz should be given credit for this invention; but it must also be noted that neither of the two models in which the distinguished geometer sought to apply his ideas, in 1694 and 1704, ever worked in practice. *Figure 11* shows the essential part of the mechanism of Leibniz's first machine, now in the Hanover Library;[60] the second machine has vanished.

The idea of using a drum gear with nine unequal length teeth is found again in other attempts, some better than others, made by the Wurtemburg priest M. Hahn[61] (1774), Lord Mahon, Earl of Stanhope[62] (1775), the Hessian military engineer J. H. Muller[63] (1784) (see *Figure 14*), the Polish

Figure 11

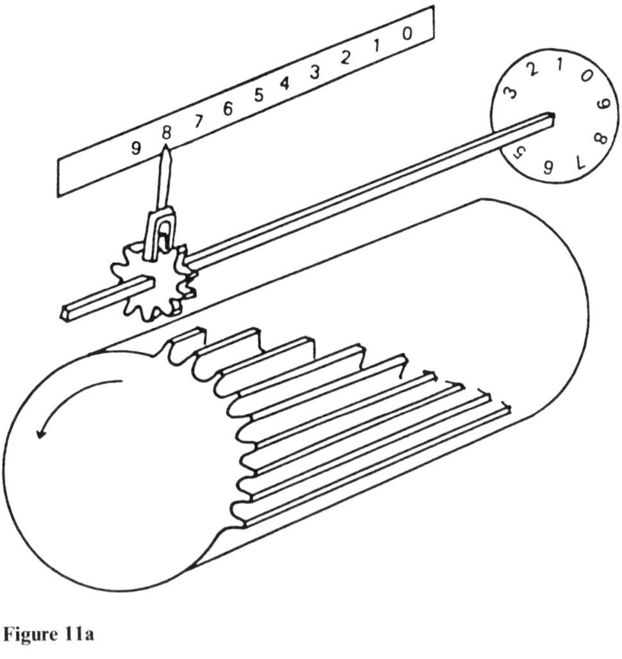

Figure 11a

Figure 12

clockmaker S. Stern[64] (1814), and by one of his compatriots, J. A. Steffel[65] (1845).

It was, however, only in 1820 that the same idea occurred to the financier Thomas de Colmar (who most probably had no knowledge of the earlier attempts), and this led to the birth of the now classic *arithmometer*, which is the first example of a truly industrial calculating machine[66] (*Figure 12*). While we do not wish to go into great detail concerning this machine, we feel that we must draw attention to its main characteristics, which have inspired a number of similar provisions, perfected to a greater or less extent, in machines built subsequently.

In order to cause the gear connected to the figure wheel to engage with the drum gear at the required point, the figure wheel gear can be moved along the length of the square-section axle by means of which its rotation is transmitted to the number wheel. A knob, fixed to the figure wheel gear, slides in a slot carrying a scale numbered from 0 to 9, arranged so that in the position numbered n the wheel engages with n teeth of the drum gear.[67] All that is necessary, therefore, is that the knobs be moved in their slots (which can be seen in *Figure 12*) to the positions corresponding to the successive digits of a number, and then a single turn of the handle (located to the right of the slots) will add this number into the total in the register subject only to the operation of the carry mechanism. If the handle is given m turns, the product of the number by m will be added to the register.

We should note here that the nine teeth on each drum occupy only about half of the periphery of the drum. This allows the carry mechanism to be operated during the period when the nontoothed part is passing below the figure wheel gear, and, consequently, the carry operation is made independent of the main movement. This independence of the carry operation is a feature of almost all machines having a setting mechanism, the exceptions being those, like Tchebichef's machine, that use a differential train to perform the carries.

By causing each drum gear to give a small displacement to its successor, the carries can be propagated successively. This is a matter of the greatest importance, first to avoid the considerable physical effort, which would otherwise be needed, when carries have to be made in several positions during a single cycle of the machine (e.g., 7548 + 4778 = 12,326), but above all to deal with a succession of carries, each made necessary by the one preceding it (e.g., 99,999 + 1 = 100,000). It is in this respect that Pascal's machine is superior to Leibniz's, in which there is no provision for this displacement.

In order that a multiplication by a number of several digits can be made without having to make that same number of turns of the handle, the product register is attached to a frame that can be moved, with respect to the fixed part of the machine, in steps of length equal to the distance between adjacent figure wheels. *For each decimal position* the multiplicand can then be added into the product register a number of times equal to the number of units in the corresponding digit of the multiplier. This means that *the total number of handle turns required is only the sum of the digits of the multiplier*. Thus, to multiply the number set in the fixed part of the machine by, for example, 365, only 14 turns of the handle have to be made instead of the 365 that would be needed if the product register were fixed with respect to the rest of the machine.

The movable frame has a second set of windows, smaller than those in which the result is read, in which a special counter wheel records the number of handle turns made in each decimal position. The multiplier can thus be read, as a check, through these windows at the end of the operation.

To change the action of the machine from addition to subtraction, all that is required is to reverse the direction of rotation of the figure wheels. To do this there exists, on each of the square-section axles, two bevel gears of opposite angles, and the simple movement of a lever (which can be seen at the left of the numbered slots in *Figure 12*) brings either one or the other into mesh with the gear that transmits the rotation to the corresponding figure wheel.[68] Now, of course, if the dividend has first been placed in the product register and the divisor subtracted as many times as possible in each decimal position, the quotient will be seen in the handle turn counter and the remainder in the product register.

A very simple zeroizer is formed by a rack that engages with gears attached to the figure wheels. Each gear has nine full-length teeth, corresponding to the digits 1 to 9, and lacks a tooth in the position corresponding to 0. As a consequence, if the rack is pulled in the direction of its length, it will turn each figure wheel until the 0 appears in the corresponding window. The figure wheels can not be returned to zero unless the movable frame is raised slightly.

A special device called a *Maltese Cross*, similar to that of the same name used in clock mechanisms,[69] prevents the rotating elements from being driven by their inertia to continue beyond the point where they should stop. Its effect is to halt the rotation in the required position, at the precise moment when this is reached, by means of a brake piece being brought into action by another part of the mechanism.

Thomas's arithmometer has been the prototype for a whole series of machines that have incorporated a variety of improvements; we shall not go into the details here, but shall simply give a short account of a few that stand out because of some particularly interesting feature.

First there is Maurel's arithmometer, called the *Arithmaurel*[70] (*Figure 13*), originally produced in 1849 and improved since then by Jayet. Here the multiaxial product register is arranged in a semicircle, so that all the figure wheels can be driven by a single drum gear having nine teeth of unequal lengths. This machine has a very delicate mechanism, similar to that used in clocks, which makes its use extremely simple. When the digits of the multiplicand have been set on the graduated sliding rods, visible in the upper part of the machine, all that needs to be done is to set the digits of the multiplier by means of the pointers on the lower dials and the product can be read from the windows in the middle of the machine. This can be summarized by saying that the mere entering of the digits of the multiplier and the multiplicand is sufficient for the product to be formed. The very delicacy of the mechanism, however, makes the machine rather fragile and not suited to continuous use; i.e., it is not an industrial machine.

The use of a central nine-toothed drum gear occurs again, in a most ingenious form, in the machine due to Tchebichef dating from 1882.[71] We have already discussed how the product register of this machine was constructed and how it can be used for simple operations. In order to adapt this to the rapid execution of multiplications and divisions the distinguished inventor has added to it a *detachable* setting mechanism, which can

Figure 13

be attached very easily whenever it is needed. Thanks to a mechanism, the details of which need not concern us here,[72] if the multiplier digits have been set by means of the knobs moving in the graduated circular slots in the front cylinder, all that needs to be done is to turn the handle until these knobs have all returned to 0:[73] the product can then be read in the windows of the product register.

By giving the arithmometer a completely circular form the English inventor J. Edmondson has made it possible to continue indefinitely, if one wishes, a division that does not come out exactly.[74]

In the machine due to Duschanek,[75] a single turn of the handle brings the three sets of digits (multiplier, multiplicand, and product) to zero at the same time. Further, in this machine all three sets of digits are set in a straight line.

Among the most recent machines derived from Thomas's arithmometer we may mention the following: the *Unitas* machine, in which the provision of a second product register enables the sum of any products, formed successively in the first product register, to be found; the *Fournier Calculator* with a multiplying handle, upon which each one-ninth of a turn gives a complete turn to the gears of the setting mechanism so that a single turn of this handle, through a greater or lesser angle, suffices in any decimal position (for example, 5 ninths of a turn, then 6 ninths of a turn, then 3 ninths suffice for a multiplication by 365); and finally the *Madas* machine, which has many improvements in detail, especially a device that makes division entirely automatic. This automatic division feature works as follows: the dividend is set in the counter register and the divisor is entered into the setting mechanism (a set of sliding knobs on the top plate); the machine then subtracts the divisor from the left part of the dividend until a negative result is obtained, which is shown as a complement. At this instant, the machine, *informed* of this result by a trigger action caused by the passage of the last figure wheel on the left from 0 to 9, reverses its direction so as to add back the divisor once (having subtracted it once too many times), and moves the carriage one place to the left and begins to subtract the divisor again as before; the cycle is repeated as often as necessary to the end of the division. The quotient is read in a counter that records the number of full revolutions, the number of times an addition has taken place being subtracted from the number of subtractions the machine has performed. Another improvement in the Madas is the provision of a complete keyboard by means of which the setting of the digits becomes much easier.

The Monroe machine, on the other hand, also uses drum gears with teeth of unequal lengths, but with only four such teeth. This enables the digit 0, 1, 2, 3, or 4 to be set by moving a small gear along the axis of the drum, as in the other machines, while another sector carrying five teeth of equal length can be added to the four-toothed drum gear, making it possible to give rotations of 5, 6, 7, 8, or 9 units.

Thanks to this arrangement, the bulk of the driving mechanism can be greatly reduced, to the extent that with the normal spacing between the rows of keys (of the order of 3/4 English inches, or about 19 mm) it is easy to accommodate both the drum gear with the four unequal length teeth and the complementary sector with the five teeth.

The adder, being of the uniaxial reversible type, allows subtractions and consequently divisions to be made by reversing the direction in which the handle is turned. Resetting to zero is done by rotating the axis common to all the number wheels.

1.2.3.2: Gears with a Variable Number of Teeth

We have seen that in order to give each figure wheel the required fraction of a full rotation there must be some way of limiting the number of teeth on the gears of the setting mechanism that engage with the gears that turn the figure wheels' axes. In the method just described this number of teeth varied from one section to another along the length of the cylinder forming the body of the drum gear. This cylinder can be reduced to a single thin disk if a way can be found to cause a variable number of teeth to protrude from its edge.

The idea of such a method, first put forward by Poleni in 1709, seems to have been applied successfully for the first time in 1841 by Dr. Roth in his circular machine[76] (*Figure 14*). Roth's very ingenious scheme was to have each setting mechanism consist of a disk with nine radial slots in its face. In each of these slots a tooth can slide; a tongue projects laterally from each tooth and is pressed toward the center of the disk by a spring. An eccentric pressing on these tongues can overcome the spring force and displace any number of teeth far enough from the center for them to protrude from the edge of the disk (*Figure 15*).

Around 1875 the Swedish inventor Odhner designed a much more robust form of variable toothed gear. In this design the displacement of the teeth along the radial slots was determined not by the action of a cam on tongues fixed to the teeth and held by a spring, but by engaging the tongues in a circular groove having two parts of unequal radii (*Figure 16*). This groove is formed in the outer part of the disk on which there is a finger, by means of which it can be turned with respect to the central part, so that the desired number of teeth are caused to project. Because of the small volume required by a gear of this design, Odhner was able to use it for a uniaxial setting mechanism and, in so doing, set a standard for this type of machine, different versions of which have been produced by several manufacturers, all incorporating certain improvements. Among these versions we may quote the *Dactyle*, made by the Chateau company, which is the most widely used machine in France (*Figure 17*). Among the improvements embodied in this machine is an extremely ingenious means for counterbalancing the inertia of the moving parts so as to prevent them from overshooting the

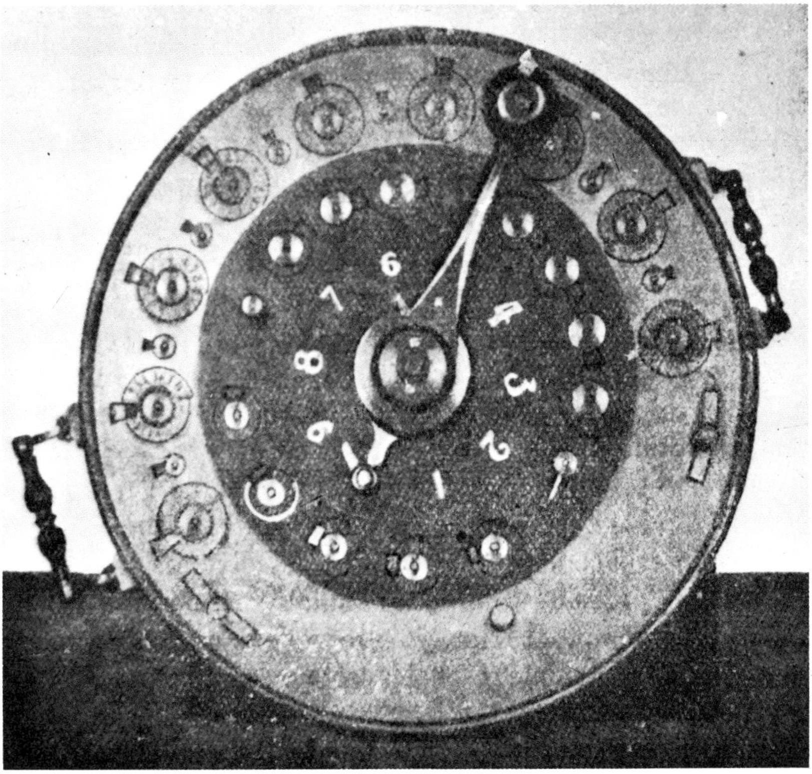

Figure 14

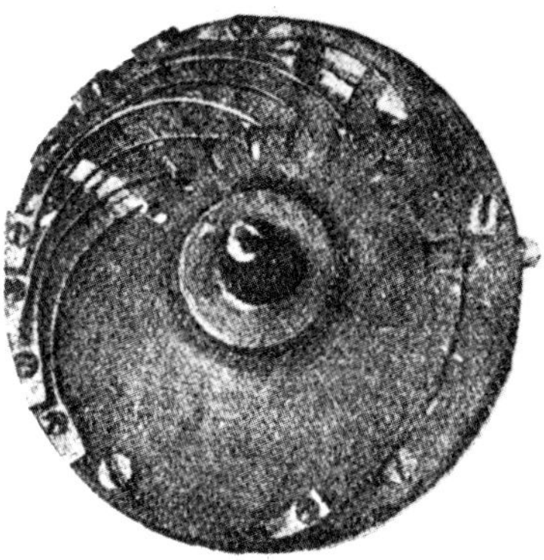

Figure 15

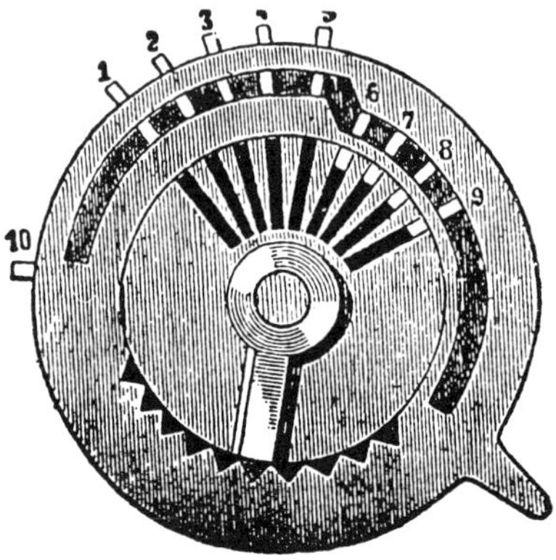

Figure 16

Figure 17

positions in which they should stop. This has made it possible to operate the machine at a much higher speed than would otherwise have been possible.

The variable toothed gear is an essential component of several German machines, notably those due to Buttner (1888), Esser (1892), and Kuttner (1894). Buttner's machine,[77] although derived from the Odhner type from which it gets its ability to perform subtraction by simply reversing the direction in which the handle is turned, has more of the external appearance of Thomas's arithmometer. It has the peculiarity, however, that the figures of the multiplicand are shown not by the positions of the studs that can be moved in numbered slots, but in a set of windows arranged in a straight line, the product register also being visible through a line of windows.[78]

Esser's machine[79] and that of Kuttner[80] (at least for the *Duplex* type) have carry mechanisms in both the multiplier and the quotient registers, which can be of advantage in certain operations, though not for multiplication or division.

A machine of a similar type was built in the United States of America under the name of *Baldwin Calculator*.

One machine belonging to the Odhner class was provided with a mechanism that enabled it to print. This machine, the Trinks *Arithmolyp*, has metal sectors containing printing characters that are driven by special toothed sectors so as to bring the figures, identical with those in the product register, into line in front of a roll of paper. At the appropriate moment, an inked ribbon is interposed and the paper roll is pressed against these figures.

Quite recently a new method for making a variable toothed gear has been devised in which the teeth that are not to be used are raised from the plane in which the contact with the driven gears occurs, instead of being made to sink into the body of the gear. This scheme is found in the Kuhrt machine (*Figure 18*), in which the teeth are pivoted about a small axle and can take up either of two positions, one in the plane of the gear and the other at an angle to this plane so as to avoid meshing with the corresponding driven gear. Each tooth has a projection at a different point on its length, arranged so that an inclined plane can cause any number of teeth between 1 and 9 to project during the course of one rotation. A second inclined plane returns all the teeth to the inactive position at the end of the rotation.

An advantage of this newer design is that it enables the mechanisms that set the number of active teeth in each column (the inclined planes) to remain fixed during the rotation; this, in turn, makes it possible to display

Figure 18

the numbers thus set, and also to set them by means of a full keyboard, as we have seen was done in the Madas machine.

1.2.3.3: Variable Motion Drive Mechanisms

Instead of designing a drive mechanism as a device whose structure is variable but that always goes through the same motions, as is the case with all machines so far described, we could consider a form in which the structure was constant but the course of action varied so as to produce the different rotations required. According to M. Mehmke this idea is seen first in an adding machine due to Leupold[81] (1727) and later in the second of the machines built by Lord Mahon[82] (1777). Among the modern machines in which the principle is used we may quote those of Dietzschold[83] (1877) and Fr. Weiss[84](1893).

The general form of Dietzschold's machine recalls the Thomas arith-

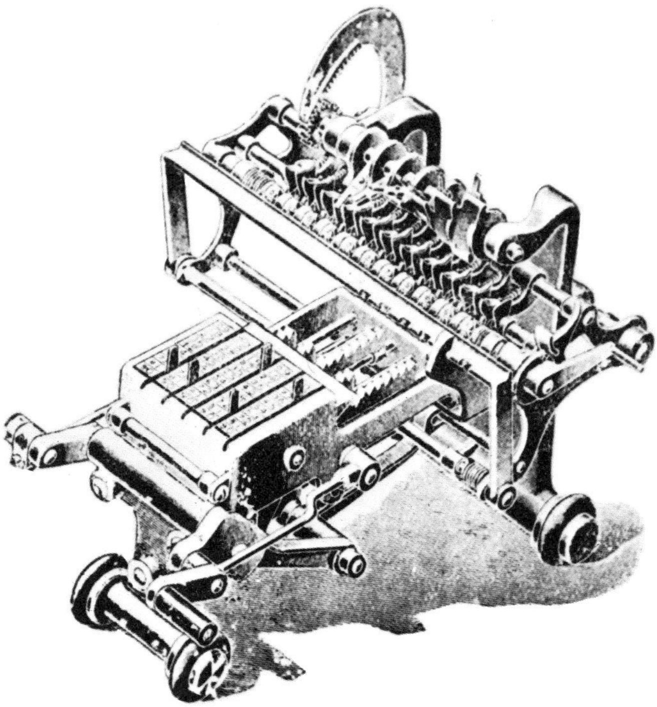

Figure 19

mometer, from which it has copied several components; but the means by which the figure wheels are caused to make the required fractions of a turn are very different. Instead of the drum gear with nine teeth of unequal length there is a ratchet wheel driven by a pawl, and a sector that can turn about the axis so as to cause the pawl to be in contact with anywhere from one to nine teeth of the ratchet wheel.

The American machine built by Grant[85] (1871) has some very original features. It consists essentially of a series of parallel racks (*Figure 19*) engaging with gears fixed to the figure wheels. The racks are fixed rigidly to a carriage that, driven by two cranks, can slide along two supporting bars and makes a complete forward and return motion when the driving handle is given one full turn. Vertical fingers can be set to positions numbered from 0 to 9 on slots in the front plate of the machine, so as to cause each rack to engage from 0 to 9 teeth with the corresponding figure wheel. This engaging takes place during the forward movement of the the carriage, and on the return movement a cam lifts the gears out of contact with the racks as well as allowing the successive carries to take place. The machine is not adapted to subtraction, which has therefore to be done by the method of complements. The figure wheels are returned to zero by means of a handle, which can be seen in *Figure 19* at the right hand end of the shaft carrying these wheels. The inventor has completed his machine by adding special equipment for printing the results.

A very unusual machine was designed by Professor Sellers[86] of the University of Wurtzburg in 1886, embodying some devices already found in other machines and other devices that are quite novel. In this machine, as in Grant's, the figure wheels are driven by racks engaging with gears while the carry mechanism, as in Tchebichef's machine, operates continuously by means of an epicyclic gear train, with the consequence that the digits of the result have to be read along an undulating line. The multiplicand is set by means of keys, as in the American adding machines, and, like Grant's machine, can print the results. Some of the mechanical provisions, however, are entirely original; one that calls for special mention is the use of the jointed lozenge or lazy-tongs linkage known as the *Nuremburg Scissors*.

The machine consists of two distinct parts that are linked during the calculation: the scissors mechanism together with the keyboard and racks, and the set of gears and figure wheels. The digits of the multiplicand are represented by the various crossing points of the scissors; for each decimal position the rack is connected to the appropriate intersection by pressing the numbered key in the corresponding column of the keyboard. The scissors are then opened, to an extent determined by the digit of the multiplier, by moving an index to the appropriate notch in a ruler numbered from 1 to 5. A multiplier greater than 5 must be dealt with as two numbers, each less than or equal to 5. Pulling on a ring returns the system to zero.

Some machines have been designed to meet special needs. Mr. Wadsworth[87] has constructed one that will only multiply or divide by π, based on the continued fraction approximation of this number.

Variable motion drivers are used in the great majority of the modern printing calculators, which form an important class of machines having a setting mechanism. They are also used in the machines of the two classes described previously, in particular, in the *Marchant*, *Demos*, and *Mercedes*.

In the Marchant the driver is a disk carrying a toothed sector, of about

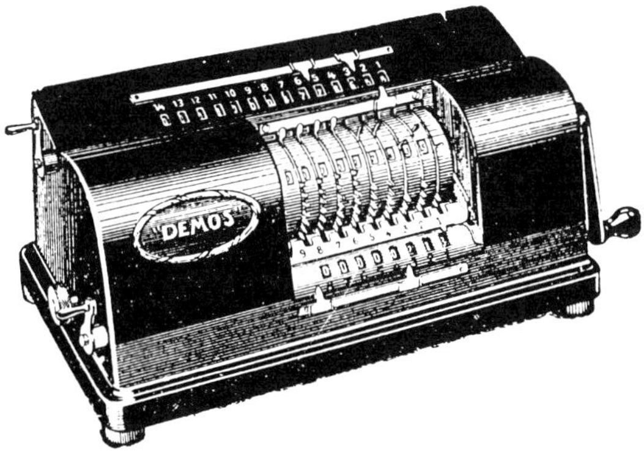

Figure 20

1/6 of the circumference of the disk, capable of being displaced along its central radius with respect to the disk by a distance a little greater than one-quarter of the height of the teeth. This sector has a roller running in a channel cut in a second disk in the form of two circular arcs of different radii joined by a short ramp, similar to that used in Odhner's variable toothed gear described earlier. Depending on the roller being in the arc of greater or lesser radius, the sector can or cannot engage with the corresponding gear; the number of teeth engaging with this gear being determined by the position of the second disk when the roller moves into the larger arc.

In machines of another type the driver performs an alternating movement. It can have the form of either a sector or a rack, the rack being considered as a sector of infinite radius. During the first phase, usually the outward movement, there is no contact between the sector and the figure wheel; this is brought about by moving the entire set of figure wheels, all mounted on a single axis, about a parallel axis, a movement that enables the contact to be broken or reestablished at will. Thus, in the Demos machine (*Figure 20*), the driver is a toothed sector that can be turned with respect to a setting disk mounted on the same axis. A digit can be set by moving the sector in such a way that the number of teeth engaging with the meshing wheel during its forward rotation (the amplitude of which is fixed at a value well below a complete turn) is equal to the digit being set. The figure wheels are moved out of contact with the drivers when the latter return to their initial positions.

Figure 21

The machine is operated by giving a full turn to the handle, cams inside the machine changing this motion to alternating motions of less than a full turn. The return to zero is brought about by means of a friction drive acting on the common axis of the figure wheels.

The driver in the Mercedes machine is a rack of an unusual type. Instead of one rack being provided for every decimal position, there are only ten; each rack, which can be used in any decimal position, sets a different number on the figure wheels. The racks are linked together in such a way that their respective movements can be either of 0, 1, 2, . . . , 9 teeth or of 9, 8, 7, . . . , 0 teeth depending on whether the machine has been set for either addition or subtraction. This enables subtraction to be done by means of complements without the operator needing to set these on the keys.

Multiplication on this machine is automatic, as is division, the method used differing little from that of the Madas.

Finally, variable motion drive mechanisms can be constructed in which the movement and the contact with the gears driving the figure wheels take place at different times.

In a full keyboard machine, such as the Burroughs (*Figure 21*), Ellis, Wales, Barrett, Continental, Victor, Corona, etc., pressure on a key has the direct effect, often brought about by the key shank itself, of causing a stop to be placed in the path of the toothed sector. In reduced keyboard machines, such as the Sundatrand, Dalton, Astra, etc., there is a small internal carriage, called the *intermediate carriage*, where the number to be set is recorded as a set of stops to be moved into the paths of the sectors at the appropriate moment. As in the case of the other reduced keyboard machines described earlier (e.g., typewriters provided with adding machinery) the setting is done in the order in which the digits would be written.

These various machines are generally provided with keys marked *Total* and *Subtotal* by means of which the contents of the totalling register can be printed, with or without returning it to zero. There is also a *Nonadd* key to allow numbers to be printed without being added to the total, this key disengaging the sectors from the adding mechanism during their movement, as well as a *Repeat* key, which allows the same number to be entered several times in succession without the operator having to reset it on the keyboard. Multiplication, already greatly simplified by the repeat key, is made even easier on some machines by a device that enables the decimal position of the multiplicand to be changed. This movement is done in the Barrett machine by moving the sum register with respect to the toothed sectors, in the Burroughs Class 4 machine by automatically shifting the numbers on the keyboard, and in reduced keyboard machines by a shift of the complete intermediate carriage.

The Patterson cash registers currently used in many of the Paris stores are full keyboard machines either with setting mechanisms of the type we have described or of a mixed type. In the second case, some of their operations are done directly without the intervention of a setting mechanism, while others require this facility. These machines are configured for the specialized addition operations encountered in sales and accounting; some can show several different totals and some can even print receipts.

Devices called *statistical* machines can be connected to some of the above-mentioned mechanisms; these are, for example, the Powers, the Samas, and the Hollerith machines. Here the effect of entering a number on the keyboard is not to record the number directly in the machine but to cause a card to be punched in such a way that it, with others, can be sorted mechanically in order to produce various classifications. After they have been grouped into classes the cards are put into a special machine that translates the perforations into a form that can be read and printed, just as a mechanical piano translates into music the perforations on a pianola roll.

1.2.3.4: Machines Capable of Direct Multiplication

In all the preceding machines multiplication and division were performed by repeated additions or subtractions in each decimal position. Each of these additions or subtractions required one turn of the handle, except for Fournier's calculator, where, as was noted, only one-ninth of a turn is required. If these repetitions are to be avoided a multiplication table must be used, and it is natural to inquire whether a machine can be built so as to use this table in a way similar to its use when doing calculations by hand. It is a remarkable fact that such a machine was built, using the most ingenious mechanisms, for the first time in France by a young inventor only 18 years old, the same age at which Pascal invented his adding machine. This was Léon Bollée, who, from that time on, has played such an important part in the creation and development of the automobile industry. His calculating machine was first demonstrated to the public at the International Exhibition of 1889.

Recent historical research has shown, however, that others were working along the same lines before Bollée. The celebrated American inventor D. E. Felt has discovered that, in 1872, a fellow American, E. D. Barbour, took out a patent for a machine that would multiply directly by means of a mechanical multiplication table. Barbour's machine was to have been constructed quite differently from Bollée's and, in any event, seems never to have been built, at least so far as has been shown by the enquiries that Mr. Felt willingly undertook at our request. Barbour's ideas had apparently been entirely forgotten and Mr. Felt's resurrection of the patent had the effect of something like a new discovery on the specialists who had some knowledge of this type of machine.[88]

Still more recently Mr. L. Leland Locke has found a curious direct multiplying machine in the US patent Office among some old models that were to be thrown away as rubbish. This model was built in 1878 by its inventor, Ramon Verea, and is of a type that is closer in concept to the machine of Bollée than to that of Barbour. Verea's mechanical realization of the multiplication table takes the form of cylinders containing holes of different diameters into which conical needles can be inserted to different depths, the projecting parts playing exactly the same role as the tongues of different lengths in the calculating plates of Bollée's machine.

It goes without saying that a man so young as Bollée, when he invented his machine, could not have had the slightest idea of these earlier attempts.

In Bollée's machine[89] (*Figure 22*) the figure wheels are turned by racks

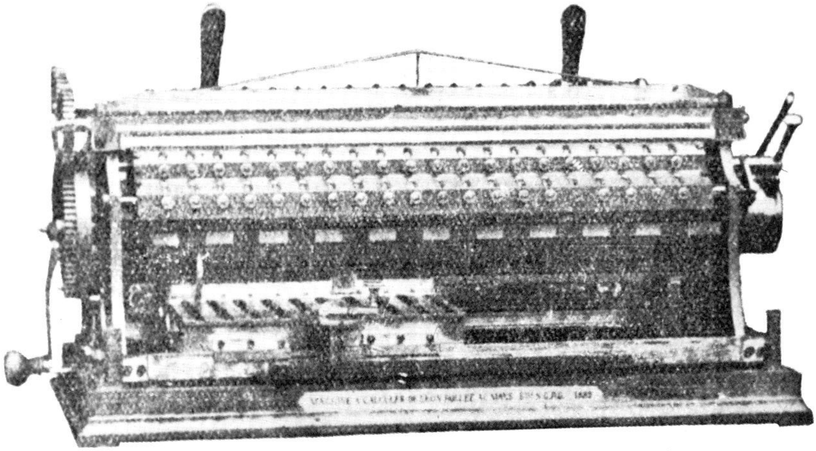

Figure 22

whose displacements are controlled by tongues fixed in plates that form, in a sense, a mechanical representation of the multiplication table. These plates are located below extensions to the racks and give them the displacement that is required for the figure wheels to turn through the the desired number of units.

As in the classical multiplication table, each plate (*Figure 23*) has nine rows and nine columns. At the intersection of each row and column the product that would be written in the table is represented by a pair of tongues fixed normally to the plate, whose lengths are equal to the numbers of steps of the rack that are needed to set the tens and the units digit of this product. Thus, if a horizontal plate is raised a distance equal to nine steps of the rack, each rack will move forward by a number of steps equal to the number represented by the tongue below its extension.

For example, at the intersection of row 7 and column 8 are two tongues of length 5 and 6; the racks above these will move through 5 and 6 steps, respectively, and turn two consecutive figure wheels through 5 and 6 units.

A number of these calculating plates are arranged on a movable carriage in such a way that, at each position in which the carriage can stop, each plate is in the interval between two consecutive figure wheels. The required row of each plate is moved to the plane of the corresponding rack by means of a stud that can be moved in one of the numbered slots of the setting

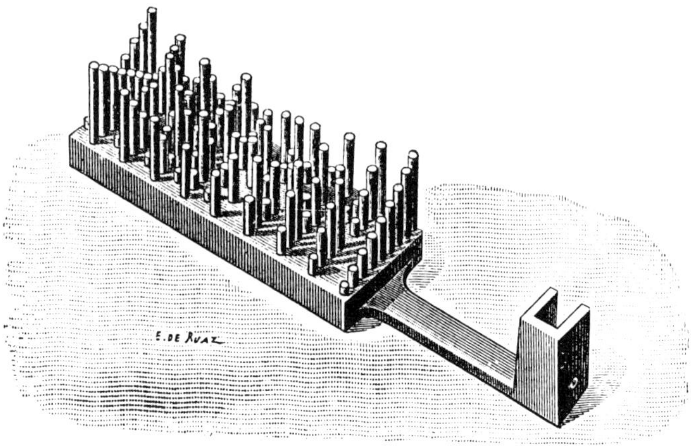

Figure 23

mechanism, exactly as in the arithmometer. To bring the required column under the rack a lever is moved so that the pointer on a numbered dial indicates the corresponding digit of the multiplier. With the plates in position, *one turn* of the handle on the side of the machine[90] adds the partial product of the multiplicand by the multiplier digit to the product register. This partial product is formed, as we have seen, by means of the mechanical multiplication table.

Let us take the example, used several times already, of multiplying by 365. The machine having been set to zero and the carriage in its initial position, the figure 3 is set by moving the lever with the right hand and the handle given a single turn with the left hand; the figure 6 is then set in the same way and the handle given another turn, and finally the 5 followed by one turn. The number of turns of the handle is thus equal to the number of digits in the multiplier instead of the sum of these digits as with the machines described earlier. In this example only three turns are needed instead of $3 + 6 + 5 = 14$.

It will be clear that if the lever is fixed to position 1 on the dial, then the machine operates as a simple adder.

There are many other mechanical details that will not be described here, such as the provision of the lever to change the direction of motion so as to change from addition to subtraction, and the ingenious method for returning the counters to zero by the use of a pair of handles that can be seen (in

Figure 22) projecting from the top of the machine. We must, however, add that Léon Bollée built a new model of his machine in 1893 that incorporates improvements of the greatest interest, in particular, a comprehensive set of interlocks so that, in the words of General Sebert, "the machine absolutely refuses to perform an impossible or logically wrong calculation, even if the operator tries to make it do so. It is equally impossible to make a wrong movement, the locking mechanism ensuring that one can only follow the correct sequence while allowing one complete freedom to perform any calculation that does not contradict theory." The interlocks enable division and extraction of square roots to be performed entirely automatically.

Tests have shown that the machine can, in one hour of normal use, perform 100 division, 120 square root calculations, and 250 multiplications, with the following numbers as the maximum ranges:

$$100{,}000{,}000{,}000{,}000{,}000{,}000/1{,}000{,}000{,}000 = 100{,}000{,}000{,}000,$$
$$\sqrt{1{,}000{,}000{,}000{,}000{,}000{,}000} = 1{,}000{,}000{,}000,$$
$$1{,}000{,}000{,}000 \times 10{,}000{,}000{,}000 = 10{,}000{,}000{,}000{,}000{,}000{,}000.$$

It can calculate 4000 terms of an arithmetic progression for which the constant increment does not exceed 10 milliards and almost the same number of squares of integers up to 100 quintillion.[91]

Mr. Malassis has made a very ingenious use of Bollée's calculating tongues. He fixed them to the surface of a cylindrical core that could be turned about its axis (according to the digit of the multiplicand) and simultaneously displaced in the direction of this axis (according to the decimal order of this digit); the tongues then act on racks mounted on a carriage and cause the figure wheels to be turned by the required number of units. The inventor has also devised a novel and most ingenious method for making the carries. Unfortunately, all that exists, so far, of this interesting machine is a wooden model made by the inventor himself.

It was not until almost the end of the last century that two machines having direct multiplication appeared as commercial products, and these are still the only ones available at present: the *Millionaire*, invented by O. Steiger in 1892, made by the Egli Company in Switzerland, and the Moon-Hopkins, made in America, first by the company of that name and later by Burroughs (*Figure 24*).

An improvement common to these two machines, which has simplified them considerably in comparison with their predecessors, is the replacement of the set of calculating plates, originally one for each decimal order

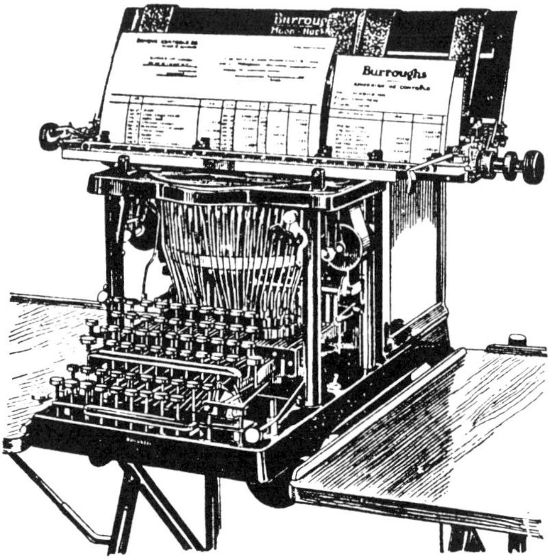

Figure 24

and each an embodiment of the complete multiplication table, by a single such plate together with a distribution mechanism. In the Millionaire this distribution mechanism consists of ten parallel equidistant thin plates or racks by means of which the required numbers can be supplied to each decimal position, as in the Mercedes machine. The Burroughs-Moon-Hopkins machine, on the other hand, has one rack for each decimal position. The multiplying element in this machine consists of a set of slotted plates, one for the units digit and one for the tens of each column of the multiplication table.

Making use of the properties of electricity, E. Selling in 1894 built a multiplying machine of a new type; in this, electromagnets were arranged in such a way that switches corresponding to the digits of the multiplicand and multiplier closed circuits, which caused the digits of the partial products to be formed.

Mr. Augustin Sequin, a descendant of the famous inventor of the tubular boiler and himself the author of a number of inventions (the most notable being a widely used mechanical speed indicator), has been so good as to give us an experimental model[92] of a multiplying machine based on a principle that seems to us to be completely novel. It is a most ingenious translation into mechanical action of a method known as *ordered multi-*

plication. This makes use of the rule for multiplying algebraic polynomials, treating the digits of the two factors as coefficients of a polynomial that represents these two numbers as powers of 10. The mechanical components designed by Mr. Seguin for his machine seem to us to have no counterparts in existing machines. It seems most imperative that this work should lead to the construction of a definitive model.

1.2.4: Machines with Complex Operations

1.2.4.1: Difference Machines

We say that an arithmetical machine is one having complex operations when it can do more than perform isolated simple arithmetical operations. Among such machines we shall consider first the *difference machines*, that is, machines that use the fact that the n th-order differences of a polynomial of degree n are constant in order to calculate successive values of a polynomial for values of the variable increasing in arithmetic progression.[93] As this is only a question of arranging mechanically for a series of additions to be made in a certain order, it is clear that there is an a priori possibility that such a machine can be built.

It appears that J. H. Muller was the first to have the idea of a machine of this type[94] in 1786, but he never built one. The same idea occurred quite independently to the English mathematician Charles Babbage in 1812, with whom, after a series of investigations made between 1823 and 1833, it became a reality in the form of a machine working with second differences.[95]

Unaware[96] of Babbage's design, the Swedish engineer Georg Scheutz formulated a proposal for a machine to work with fourth differences. He submitted this to the Académie des Sciences de Paris[97] in September 1838, but did not succeed in building the machine, with the help of his son Edward, until 1853. The machine (*Figure 25*) has figure wheels arranged in five stages corresponding, from the highest to the lowest, to the values of the polynomial and those of the first, second, third, and fourth differences, respectively. The position of each wheel specifies the number of units by which the transfer mechanism must turn the wheel immediately above, the mechanism acting alternately on the even and odd stages and turning the wheels on one stage by the numbers of units shown on those of the stage below. The process is started by setting the respective stages to the values of $u_2, \Delta u_1, \Delta^2 u_1, \Delta^3 u_0, \Delta^4 u_0$, the last difference being constant. After the first operation of the transfer mechanism the values of $\Delta^3 u_1$ and Δu_2 replace

Figure 25

those of $\Delta^3 u_0$ and Δu_1, respectively, the numbers in the odd-order stages remaining unchanged. The second operation acts on these numbers (odd-order stages) and replaces $\Delta^2 u_1$ by $\Delta^2 u_2$ and u_2 by u_3 and so on.[98]

The first eight digits, reading from the left, of the uppermost stage (i.e., the values of the polynomial) are stamped on a strip of lead so as to form a plate for stereotype printing. Thus the machine provides not only for the calculation of tables but also for their printing, avoiding errors of both calculation and transcription. It also results in a considerable saving of time, for it has been stated that the machine can calculate and print two-and-a-half pages of figures in the time it would take a good compositor to set up a single page.

Thanks to the generosity of a rich American merchant, Mr. J. F. Rathbone, the Scheutz machine that was displayed at the 1855 Paris Exhibition became the property of the Dudley Observatory at Albany in the United States, where it has been used to calculate tables of logarithms, natural sines, and logarithmic sines.[99]

Another copy of this machine was ordered by the British Government and installed in the offices of the Registrar General in Somerset House, London, in 1858. This machine was constructed by the firm of Bryan Donkin, who introduced several improvements in the details. This machine calculated and printed 605 tables, of large quarto size, which formed the basis for the British Post Office Savings Bank's calculations of annuity premiums.[100]

Another Swedish engineer, Martin Wiberg, designed a difference machine to perform exactly the same calculations as Scheutz's. Because it incorporated some new mechanical devices, the physical size could be reduced significantly, as compared with the size of the Scheutz machine, which was about that of a small piano.[101] Wiberg's machine was demonstrated to the Académie des Sciences de Paris by the astronomer Delaunay,[102] who gave it his unreserved praise. It has 75 metal disks numbered from 0 to 9 on their peripheries, mounted on the same axis about which they can be turned independently by a friction drive. They form 15 groups of 5, each group corresponding to one decimal order, the first disk on the left of each group representing the digit of that order in the function to be calculated, the second disk the corresponding digit in its first difference, and so on to the fifth disk representing the digit of that order in the constant fourth difference. Thus the value calculated for the function is read by taking the digit on the first disk on the left and then, in succession, that on every fifth disk to the right.

This machine, like Scheutz's, operates first on the third and first differences and then on the second differences and the function value. In another part of the machine a mechanical linkage brings together the first eight digits of the function value and sets them on print bars from which stereo molds can be made.

The note by Delaunay, referred to above, gives a very detailed description of the mechanism without, unfortunately, any diagrams. The essential component is an axis parallel to that of the disks and carrying 30 fingers, which, when brought to a position behind certain teeth joined to the disks, push these forward and so cause the disks to turn about their common axis. A strip in which slots are cut so as to give it the form of a comb is placed so that the teeth of the 30 disks driven by the fingers can pass freely through the slots while the others are held stationary.

Wiberg's machine also has been used to calculate and print logarithmic[103] and financial tables, and has revealed errors in similar tables published previously.

Mr. G. B. Grant, the builder of one of the multiplying machines described previously, has designed a difference machine.[104] The general arrangements are the same as in Wiberg's, with numbered disks threaded on a single axis and grouped according to decimal order, but there are some special mechanical provisions, particularly in the printing part of the machine.

1.2.4.2: General Arithmetical Machines

Can one imagine a machine that could perform not merely an isolated arithmetical operation but an entire series of such operations, without any intervention by a human operator? This is the question that Babbage did not fear to attack from 1834 onward, and which he solved with the design of his *analytical engine*. In this device the numbers to be operated upon are taken from the first part of the machine, called the *store*, where they are inscribed on figure wheels stacked in columns, to the second part, called the *mill*, where they are subjected to the desired series of operations. These operations are performed mechanically according to orders issued by a *control unit*; the orders vary, of course, according to the series of operations that are to be performed, and, as the control unit makes use of perforated cards, it is not unlike the device used to control the weaving in the Jacquard loom. Babbage made all the components needed for his machine[105] but unfortunately died before he had been able to assemble them; they remain unassembled in the South Kensington Museum in London, where they can still be seen. The son of the inventor has brought together in one volume all the papers left by Babbage concerning his machine.[106]

Another solution to the same problem was obtained by the great Spanish engineer Torres Quevedo, this time using electromechanical methods. The high degree of perfection to which Mr. Torres has brought the science of automatic machinery is well known because of his remarkable chess-playing machine. This device can, in an end game in which the machine plays King and Rook against an opponent with only a King, always mate even though the opponent is at liberty to make any legal move.[107] His profound studies of this difficult subject have led the learned engineer to formulate the following completely general principle[108]: "It is always possible to build an automaton whose actions depend on a greater or lesser number of circumstances, according to rules which one can impose arbitrarily during it construction."

Since then Mr. Torres has announced his intention to build a calculator that will be *purely automatic*, able to perform any desired sequence of arithmetical operations on any numbers whatever, without the intervention of an operator, after the numbers and a statement of the operations to be performed have been given to the machine. The operations are given to the machine by means of an ordinary typewriter provided with symbols representing the four fundamental operations of arithmetic and an equal sign. Once this has been done the machine functions automatically and

Figure 26

then, in its turn using the typewriter, prints the results. The scale of such a problem defies the imagination; nevertheless Mr. Torres has given a complete solution, although, it must be said, this presents certain complications in view of the very many electrical connections it requires. Thus, as he himself has said, it should be regarded more as a scientific curiosity than as a practical proposition, but yet as of great theoretical importance.

So far Mr. Torres has built only a model, which he calls the *electromechanical arithmometer* (*Figure 26*), intended to perform a single arithmetical operation, although one of any type, as instructed by the typewriter.[109] After completing one operation the machine is again ready to accept another from the typewriter. Given a statement of a problem, it would be possible to provide the machine with a means for executing a sequence of instructions expressing a set of related operations for the solution of that problem. This would add considerable complication to the construction of the machine but would not, in principle, require anything new.

It can therefore be said that, thanks to Mr. Torres, Babbage's problem has been solved completely by means of electromechanical machinery. But even more can be said: the great Spanish inventor has taken up the problem of building a machine that will attain the same ends by purely mechanical means, yet differing completely from Babbage's design. We look forward to the day when we shall see this wonderful machine working. From now on, given the confidence we can place in its inventor, we can look to him to provide a final solution to the problem of building a general arithmetical machine.

1.2.4.3: Number Theory Machines

There are problems in number theory, such as the solution in integers of indeterminate equations in two variables (a problem reduced by Mr. André Gérardin to one of certain congruences) or finding whether or not a given large number is prime, that demand such heavy numerical work as to deter even the most strong-minded calculators. The aim of number-theoretic machines is to carry out such studies mechanically both at high speed and with perfect certainty. Several different types of machine have been proposed by Mr. Gérardin himself, who seems to have been the first to initiate studies of this type, and by Mr. Kraitchik, Mr. P. Carissan, and his brother Commandant E. Carissan.

Figure 27 shows the congruence machine built by Commandant Carissan and demonstrated by him at the exhibition held to celebrate the centenary of Thomas's arithmometer.[110] It consists of a set of concentric metal rings on which are fixed a set of equidistant steel pins, the number of pins on each ring being a prime number (the outermost ring holding 59 pins in the present machine).[111] A drive wheel and gearing causes all the rings to turn at the same time so that various pins come into radial alignment as they pass a fixed radius called the *inspection line*. Possible solutions to a given problem, with respect to a given modulus, are represented by small caps placed over certain pins. A solution is found when the alignment consists of only capped pins. This is detected by the machine in a most ingenious way: as the capped pins pass the inspection line they lift small copper hammers and these make contact in an electrical circuit; when the alignment is wholly of capped pins all the contacts are made, the current flows, and a characteristic *click* is heard in a telephone receiver held by the operator.[112]

To give some idea of the speed at which one can work when using this machine we quote some examples for which careful timings have been taken.

1. A solution in integers for $x < 10{,}000$ of $x^2 - 13y^2 = 1$.
Response: $x = 649$, $y = 180$; time: 5 minutes.

Figure 27

2. Express 708,158,977 as the sum of two squares.
Response: $19{,}224^2 + 18{,}401^2$; time: 10 minutes.

3. Find whether or not the number $2^{31} - 1$ $(=2{,}147{,}483{,}647)$ is prime.
Response: prime; time: 15 minutes.

Notes

1. See *Description du Cabinet de Sainte-Gerevièue*, by Claude de Molinet (1692), p 23, Pl. I; also *Theatrum Arithmetico-Geometricum* by J. Leupold (1727), p. 8.

2. *Rescerches sur l'Origine de l'Abaque Chinois*, by A. Vissière, in the *Bulletin de Géographie* (1892).

3. *Soroban or Japanese Abacus*, by G. Knott, *Transactions of the Asiatic Society* (1886).

4. The principle is basically the same as that employed in marking the score at billiards by sliding beads along a rod, or, more simply, in counting on the fingers.

5. Instead of a movable rule sliding along the length of a fixed rule, a perforated endless band could be used, sliding below a sheet in which there were numbered windows. This arrangement is used in *Bassett's adder*.

6. *B.S.E.,* 1828, p. 394.

7. *Description des Brevels dont la Durée est Empirée*, Vol. XXIX, p. 336.

8. It had been used previously in Perrault's machine (1666), which already had a mechanism for tens carry.

9. The observation is the following. Suppose that after moving the ruler m through a divisions we need to move it through a further b divisions and that $a + b > 10$. The units digit of the sum will be $a + b - 10$. Thus if we bring the mark on m, which is opposite that for b on f, to a position opposite that 10 mark on f, that is, if we move m back by an amount $10 - b$, then the mark on m opposite 0 on f is that corresponding to $a - (10 - b) = a + b - 10$, the required units figure. After this, all that has to be done so as to effect the carry is to advance the movable ruler for the tens by one unit.

10. See ***14***, p. 14. This instrument is in the collection of the Conservatoire des Arts et Métiers.

11. Addiator and Hora both have two faces, one for addition and the other for subtraction.

12. See ***13*** (Supplement) p. 5, and ***14***, p. 25 (***6***, p. 230).

13. See ***14***, p. 191.

14. *Cosmos*, Vol. 55, 1906, p. 566.

15. (Ed.) d'Ocagne actually called these *Ribbon's Adders*, but this was an obvious error.

16. This is in the Conservatoire des Arts et Métiers, alongside another small device for multiplication due to the same inventor, consisting of a sheet in which there are windows and which can be moved in front of a set of parallel cylinders carrying numbers.

17. (Ed.) d'Ocagne is obviously describing Napier's *Promptuarium*, but the fact that he attributes it to Bollée seems to indicate that he was not, personally, familiar with the device.

18. *B.S.E.*, 1869, p. 137. also ***6***, p. 235.

19. ***6***, p. 235.

20. *C.R.*, 30 March 1903, p. 807.

21. *P.J.*, 1877, p. 152. Also ***6***, p. 233.

22. See the report of Colonel Sebert (*B.S.E.*, 1895, p. 977).

23. There is an historical study of the origin of these machines in ***17***, giving much little-known information.

24. (Ed.) This diagram was not in the original, but has been added by the editors in order to avoid some particularly obscure wording.

25. (Ed.) d'Ocagne actually said "dividend," but this was an error.

26. (Ed.) d'Ocagne was unaware of the earlier work of Wilhelm Schickard in 1623.

27. There are four original models of this machine in the Conservatoire des Arts et Métiers. One carries the signature of Pascal himself, another a dedicatory address to the Académie des Sciences written and signed by Pascal's nephew Canon Périer, son of his sister Gilberte. Diderot gave a detailed description of the machine in the *Grande Encyclopédie* (Vol. I, p. 680), which was reproduced in the *Encyclopédie Méthodique* (Vol. I, p. 136) and also in the *Oeuvres Complètes de Pascal* (Ed. de la Hayne, Vol. IV, 1779, p. 34). The interested reader may also consult the *Receuil des Machines Approuvées par l'Académie des Sciences* (Vol. IV, p. 137). A most interesting historical note on Pascal's machine appeared over the signature of Mr. F. Bouquet in the August 1899 issue of the Rouen journal, *La Normandie* (Vol. VI, p. 385).

28. (Ed.) Pascal's machine actually connected the spoked input driving wheel to the result figure wheel by a series of peg toothed gears; the two items were not connected to the same axis.

29. (Ed.) The movement is actually started when the driving wheel is about halfway through a full turn.

30. *Machines Approuvées par l'Académe des Sciences* (Vol. IV, p. 131). We have had the opportunity to see a copy of this machine in the workshops of the Payen company, where Thomas's Arithmometer, which will be described later, was built.

31. *Machines Approuvées par l'Académe des Sciences*, Vol. V, p. 103.

32. *Description and Usage of Two Arithmetic Instruments*, London, 1673. The second instrument was designed for multiplication. Montucla, in his *Récréations Mathématiques*, thought that Morland was unaware of the Pascal machine. [(Ed.) Morland was very likely aware of the Pascal machine, see Williams, M. R., "From Napier to Lucas," *Annals of the History of Computing*, Vol. 5, Num. 3, July 1983, pp. 279–296.]

33. *Miscelanea Venetiis*, 1709, p. 27.

34. *B.S.E.*, 1843, p. 411.

35. ***14***, p. 53.

36. *Philos. Trans.*, Vol. IX, p. 438.

37. *Amer. Scient.* 1869, p. 20, and *J. Franklin Institute*, 1870, p. 8 (***6***, p. 241). This instrument, known as the *Lightning Adder*, consisted of two circles touching externally, one corresponding to the first 100 integers and the second to the hundreds. They were enclosed in a metallic cover into which they fitted exactly and in which there was a window in the region of the point of contact of the circles, in which the sum appeared. There are two copies of this instrument in the Conservatoire des Arts et Métiers. [(Ed.) It is not clear whether d'Ocagne means 0–99 or 1–100 by the phrase "the first 100 integers."]

38. ***14***, p. 65.

39. ***6*** p. 243. Threaded nuts, as in Orlin's machine, are used also in a little instrument due to Smith and Pott, limited to the additon of single digit numbers. See *Amer. Scient.* Vol. XXIII, p. 214; *P.J.*, 1876, p. 401 (***6***, p. 243, note 173).

40. *Journal des Savants*, 1751, p. 508.

41. *A.P.C.*, 3rd term 1900, p. 356.

42. In a very recently constructed machine called *Direct*, employing exactly the same principle as Tchebichef's, an extra device makes it possible to bring all the figures of the total into line.

43. ***6***, p. 243, note 175.

44. *Schweiz, Polyt. Zeitschr.*, 1866, p. 33; ***6***, p. 244, note 180; ***14***, p. 51.

45. ***6***. p. 243, note 176.

46. For this and d'Azevedo's machine see *P.J.*, Vol. CCLX, 1896, p. 262.

47. ***14***, p. 67.

48. *P.J.*, 1886, p. 263; ***14***, p. 62. The first patent was granted to Mayer in 1881 (***6***, p. 244, note 181).

49. ***6***, p. 244, note 180. This machine has five keys, for the numbers 1 to 5, and is obviously the same as described in ***14*** (p. 69) under the name *centigraphe*, but without the name of its constructor.

50. *11*, p. 19. A patent for a similar machine was granted to Mr. Cuhel in 1890. See *6*, p. 265, note 230.

51. The printing machine developed by Felt and Tarrant is called a *comptograph*. The *comptometer* does not print but shows the total through small windows at the front of the machine.

52. (Ed.) d'Ocagne is confusing here because he is talking about machines with two different operating actions. The comptometer was entirely key driven, the mere entering of a number causing it to be added to the total, while some of the other machines required that a number be entered on the keys and then a lever pulled to cause the actual addition.

53. *6*, p. 247. This machine shows the successive totals in the windows, as does the comptometer, but prints them at the same time. Mr. Malassis has shown us a wooden model, made by himself, of a machine of this type that he has designed and that has some very interesting mechanical details. One would have hoped to see a full working model.

54. *6*, p. 246, note 182.

55. *Zeitschr. für Math. und Phys.*, 1899, Supplement, p. 533 (*6*, p. 244, note 181).

56. Experiments have shown that in such circumstances the time required to multiply two 8-figure numbers can be as low as about 5 seconds—which is the duration of the six musical "pips" by means of which the TSF broadcasts the time. [(Ed.) Although this last remark is not very meaningful to the modern reader, we thought it interesting and indicative of d'Ocagne style and thus left it in the footnote.]

57. All the different uses of the comptometer are described in the excellent book *Applied Mechanical Arithmetic as Practiced on the Comptometer* (Felt and Tarrant, Chicago, 1914). An operator's guide had been published previously by H. Goldman, with the title *The Arithmachinist: A Practical Self-Instructor in Mechanical Arithmetic* (Chicago, 1898).

58. (Ed.) This figure was not in the original volume but has been added by the editors in the hope that it will make the explanation slightly clearer.

59. (Ed.) This diagram was not in the original edition but has been added by the editors.

60. *Miscell. Berolin.* 1710, p. 317; and *Leibnitii Opera*, 1768, Vol, III, No. 74. Leibniz's machine was the subject of a communication by Mr. Runge to the *Third International Congress of Mathematicians* at Heidelberg, 1904. In a review of the first edition of the present work, in *Bulletin Astronomique* (1894, p. 419), Mr. Radau gave a fairly detailed description of the machine.

61. *Deutsch-Merkur* (Wieland), May 1779, p. 137. A work has recently been dedicated to Mathieu Hahn by Mr. Engelmann (Berlin 1923).

62. *Philos. Mag.* 1885, p. 16.

63. *Deutsch-Merkur* (Wieland) March 1784, p. 269. The Muller machine is still in existence at the Darmstadt Museum. The Berlin and Munchen Technische Hochschulen both have copies of Hahn's machine, built at the beginning of the 19th century. All these machines are of the circular type.

64. *Leipz. Litteraturzeitung*, 1814, p. 244; and *Archives des Inventions et Découvertes*, Vol. VIII, p. 264. After inventing his first machine Stern designed another (1817) specially intended for calculation of square roots. He later combined the features of the two machines into a single machine of a unique type (*6*, p. 265, note 229).

65. *Tygodnik Illustrowany* 1863, p. 207 (*6*, p. 264, note 226).

66. As a result of the initiative of Malassis the centenary of the invention of Thomas's arithmometer was celebrated in Paris in June 1920; the *Société d'Encouragement pour l'Industrie National* organized a retrospective exhibition, a display of modern calculating

machines and a series of meetings related to these events. The proceedings of these meetings have been gathered together in *B.S.E.*, Vol 132 (1920), with a series of papers of the greatest interest, including the reports on the arithmometer made at various times by Francoeur, Hoyau, Benoit, and General Sebert (pp. 660, 662, 687, 694). We also owe to Hirn (*Annales de Génie Civil*, 1863) an interesting note on various uses to which the machine can be put. Slightly modified versions of Thomas's arithmometer have been built in Germany by Burkhardt and in England by Tate.

67. (Ed.) See *Figure 11a*, which has been added by the editors.

68. (Ed.) See *Figure 11a*, which has been added by the editors.

69. (Ed.) The Maltese Cross is used on the winding mechanism and was designed to prevent the spring from being unwound beyond a certain point.

70. *C.R.*, first series, 1849, and *B.S.E.* August 1849, p. 370. A very detailed description of the arithmaurel, by Lalanne, appeared in *A.P.C.* second series, 1854 p. 288.

71. See *Figure 65* in Appendix I.

72. This is given in Appendix I.

73. The number of turns of the handle was also limited automatically in the model of Thomas's arithmometer built during the period 1840–1850.

74. *Philos. Mag.* 2nd series, 1885 p. 15.

75. *Polyt. Journ.* (Dingler) 1886, p. 264 (***6***, p. 264, note 224).

76. Two examples of this machine are in the Conservatoire des Arts et Métiers.

77. ***13***, p. 151; also ***14***, p. 102; also ***6*** p. 258, note 209.

78. This was already provided in Duschanek's machine; it is found again in Steiger's machine.

79. ***6***, p. 263, note 221.

80. *P.J.*, 1896, p. 199 (***6***, p. 258 note 209).

81. *Theatrum Arith.-Geom.*, p. 38 (***6***, p. 251, note 194).

82. Vogler, *Anleitung zum Entwerfen Graphischer Tafeln*, 1877, p. 50 (***6***, ibid.).

83 ***11***, p. 40.

84. ***6***, p. 251, note 194.

85. According to an undated (but earlier than 1895) brochure published in Lexington, Massachusetts. See also *Amer. Journ. of Science and Arts*, 1874, p. 277 (***6***, p. 264, note 228). This machine should not be confused with one that another American inventor, Geo. B. Grant, demonstrated to the Franklin Institute on 19 October 1876 (*Scientific American*, 12 May 1877).

86. *Eine neue Rechenmachine*, Berlin, 1887. See also: *P.J.*, 1899 p. 193 (***6***, p. 251, note 195); ***13***, p. 152.

87. *Journal of the Franklin Institute*, 1903, p. 131.

88. Since then Mr. Malassis has found the plate, from which Barbour's patent was printed, in a case in the Conservatoire des Arts et Métiers; it had been presented by Edouard Lucas and had remained there, unknown, since 1888.

89. For more details see the report by General Sebert, in *B.S.E.*, p. 732.

90. As the lever is moved with the left hand and the handle turned with the right, there need be no interval between these two movements.

91. (Ed.) "Milliard" is presumably 10^9 and "quintillion" is 10^{18}; this latter limit is for the resultant squares and not for the integers to be squared.

92. Now housed at the Conservatoire des Arts et Métiers.

93. See the section in the Introduction dealing with the method of differences.

94. The Muller project was described in a book by P. E. Klipstein: *Beschreibung einer neu erfundenen Rechenmaschine*, Frankfurt, 1786. [(Ed.) d'Ocagne actually gave the date as 1876, but this was an error.]

95. *P.J.*, Vol. XLVII, 1832, p. 441. Babbage also wrote about his machine in *The Ninth Bridgewater Treatise* (2nd edition, London, 1838, p. 186). The primitive model of this machine is housed at the Museum of Sumerset House College. [(Ed.) The model is currently in the Science Museum, London.]

96. (Ed.) d'Ocagne appears not to know that the Scheutz team was inspired to its efforts by an untitled article, describing Babbage's machine in detail, by D. Lardner that appeared in the *Edinburgh Review*, July, 1834, Vol. LIX, Num. CXX, p. 263–327.

97. *C.R.* 2nd series, 1838, p. 1056. It was in relation to this machine that Babbage submitted a most interesting note to the same Académie (*C.R.* 2nd series, 1855, p. 577) describing a system for mechanical notation by means of which the action of any mechanism could be described in graphical terms.

98. Appendix II gives more details on the functioning of this machine; there is a full account in *P.J.*, Vol. CLIV, 1860, pp. 241–321.

99. A sample of these tables was on sale in Paris in 1858, entitled *Spécimen de Tables Calculées, Stéréotypées et Imprimées au Moyen d'une Machine*. [(Ed.) An English version was also available under the title *Specimens of Tables Calculated, Stereomoulded, and Printed by Machinery*, Longmans, London, 1857.]

100. *Tables of Lifetimes, Annuities and Premiums, with an Introduction by W. Farr*, London, 1864.

101. (Ed.) To compare the Scheutz machine with a small piano is rather misleading. The machine is a great deal smaller than almost all modern pianos and would almost, but not quite, fit inside a standard legal size file cabinet drawer. The editors have been unable to determine where this misconception originated, but it is quite common in the literature.

102. *C.R.*, 1st series, 1863, p. 330.

103. *Logarithm-Tabella, utraknade och tryckte med raknemaskin*; Stockholm, 1875.

104. *Amer. Journ. of Science and Arts*, 2nd series, 1871, p. 113.

105. (Ed.) d'Ocagne is mistaken here; Babbage had the machine planned out but never had all the components actually constructed.

106. Babbage never published anything on his invention during his lifetime. The only printed document relating to this to appear is the article by the Sardinian Engineer Captain (later General) Menebrea, published in French in the *Bibliothèque Universale de Genève*, 1842, Vol. XLI, p. 352. An English translation with the addition of very important mathematical notes was published in 1843 in *Scientific Memoirs*, Vol. III, by Ada, Lady Lovelace (the only daughter of Lord Byron), who had been taught mathematics by Mary Somerville and who signed the paper only with her initials. The model originally planned by Babbage would have had 1000 columns of 50 wheels each and therefore would have allowed 1000 numbers each of 50 digits to be employed, either as data or as results. Clearly these quantities could be reduced considerably without any difficulty arising. [(Ed.) The volume, produced by Babbage's son, Henry Provost Babbage, has been reprinted as Volume 2 in this Reprint Series for the History of Computing.]

107. A description of this machine appeared in *La Nature*, 13 June 1914, p. 56.

108. (Ed.) Rather than translate the French at this point, we have extracted the words from Torres's original paper, reproduced in B. Randell's *Origins of Digital Computers*, Springer, 1975, p. 89.

109. A detailled description of the electromechanical arithmometer, written by Mr. Torres, can be found in *B.S.E.*, Vol. 132, 1920, p. 588.

110. Described by him in *B.S.E.*, Vol. 132, 1920, p. 600.

111. (Ed.) Interested readers are referred to the more modern work of D. H. Lehmer for a fuller discussion of this type of calculating machine. Lehmer's article, "A History of the Sieve Process" (*A History of Computing in the Twentieth Century*, Ed. N. Metropolis, J. Howlett, and G. Rota, Academic Press, 1980, p. 445) provides much clearer explanations of the mode of operation of such a device.

112. Jules Carpentier had suggested a modification to this machine to aid the operator. This consists of powering the drive mechanism by a small electric motor, which will automatically stop when a solution passes under the inspection line.

Chapter II: Graphical Calculation

2.1: Graphical Arithmetic and Algebra

In attempting to solve a problem by ordinary graphical calculation, the numbers being manipulated are represented by segments of straight lines measured along a linear scale. These straight lines are then incorporated into various geometrical constructions, which eventually result in another straight line segment the length of which, again measured on a linear scale, gives the solution to the problem. In certain special cases the lengths of the segments are made proportional not to the numbers themselves but to some simple function of the numbers, such as their square or logarithm. In these cases the lengths of the lines must be measured along the corresponding functional scales. There are rare occasions in which the geometrical elements used for the operations are not line segments but angles. In these cases the magnitudes being represented are determined by readings taken from a protractor. In the great majority of cases only straight line segments and linear scales are actually used, and, with this as a basis, rules can be developed by means of which all the elementary operations of arithmetic and algebra can be reduced to operations on simple drawings.

The first attempt in this direction seems to have been made by an engineer in the Ponts et Chausées, Cousinery. His book,[1] published in Paris in 1840, can be regarded as the starting point for studies on this subject. Further refinements were made by later geometers, among the most notable of whom was Cremona.[2] Other contributors can be noted from the fairly complete accounts that have been given by several writers, particularly by Culmann in the first part of his great treatise[3] and by Favaro.[4]

Great advances were made by Massau, an engineer at the Belgian Ponts et Chaussées and a Professor at the University of Ghent. We ourselves have made an attempt to extract from the impressive mass of his publications[5] the principles that are somewhat hidden among the numerous applications but that are of the greatest interest to engineers. This task was undertaken in order to present Massau's ideas in a simpler form, more systematically organized and better adapted for teaching. This led to the course on the elements of graphical algebra that we gave for the first time at the Sorbonne in 1907[6] and later included in our lectures at the École Polytechnique.[7]

We shall not go into detail here, but only remark that a most interesting fact is that all these elements of graphical algebra, and also those of graphical integration that follow from them, are based on a single fundamental construction, which can be stated as follows (*Figure 28*):

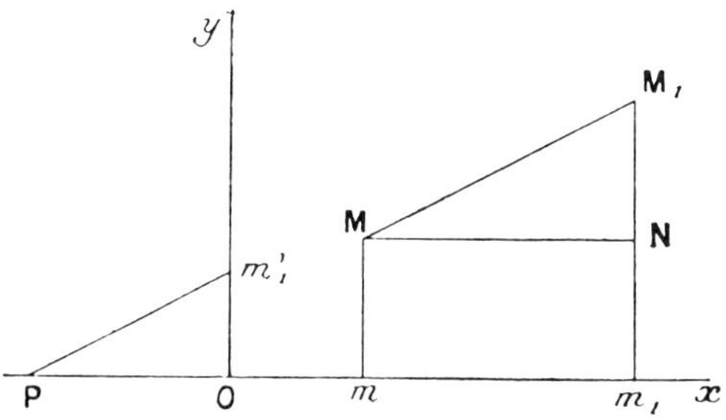

Figure 28

Let Ox, Oy be rectangular axes and let a set of reference lines be taken, parallel to Oy. Let numbers be represented by line segments in these directions with scale units μ, μ_0, μ_1, respectively, so that, for example, if the line segment mm_1 represents the number a its length is μa. Let P (the *pole* of the construction) be taken on Ox as shown in *Figure 28*, with $OP = (\mu\mu_0)/\mu_1$. Then, if numbers a_1 and z_1 are represented by mm_1 and Om'_1 respectively, and MM_1 is parallel to Pm'_1 and MN parallel to Ox, $NM_1 = \mathrm{a}_1\mathrm{z}_1$.

It follows that if we mark on Ox the line segments $m_1m_2 = a_2$, $m_2m_3 = a_3$, etc., and on Oy the segments $Om'_2 = z_2$, $Om'_3 = z_3$, etc., and construct the polygon $MM_1M_2M_3 \cdots M_n$ with sides parallel to Pm'_1, $\mathrm{P}m'_2$, $Pm'_3, \ldots, Pm'_n$, then if a is the ordinate of the final point M_n with respect to M as zero,

$$a_1z_1 + a_2z_2 + a_3z_3 + \cdots + a_nz_n = a.$$

If therefore we mark on Ox the points corresponding to the coefficients a_1, $a_2, \ldots, a_n$, then draw through these points the reference lines and mark on the first and last of these points M and M_n, respectively, so that the difference of their ordinates is a, we have what may be called a *graphical representation* of the above equation. Any polygonal line joining MM_n with intermediate vertices on the reference lines will determine, by the direction of its sides, values $z_1, z_2, \ldots, z_n$ that satisfy the equation. A further consequence is that if we apply the construction to a set of n linear equations in n unknowns, we shall have solved the set if we succeed in constructing the polygons so that all the corresponding sides have the same direction; this can be achieved with the aid of a theorem of Massau, using a method of false position.[8]

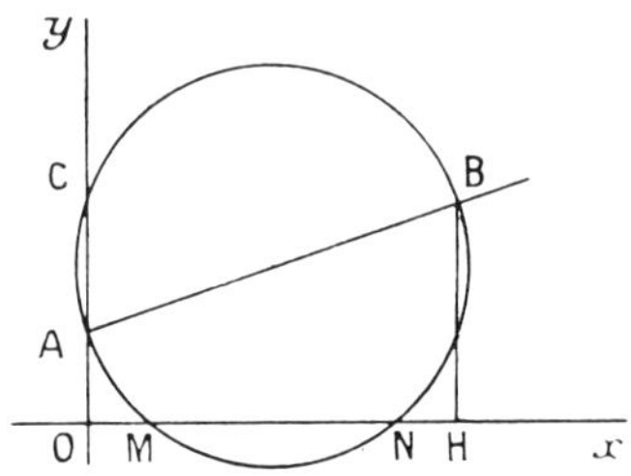

Figure 29

Another method for the solution of linear equations, based on an ingenious method of graphical elimination, has been given by Mr. Van den Berg.[9]

We have shown that Lill's method for solving algebraic equations of arbitrary degree by a fast graphical trial-and-error process can also be reduced to the same principle.[10] Thus this one idea dominates the whole of graphical algebra.

For quadratic equations for which no trial-and-error process is necessary, Lill's method can be put in the form of a very simple construction, as follows.

With rectangular axis Ox, Oy (*Figure 29*) mark on Oy the point A such that OA is the unit of length and, in terms of this unit, mark B such that $OH = -p$, $HB = q$.

The circle having diameter AB cuts Ox at points M and N such that OM and ON, again measured in terms of the unit length OA, are the roots of the equation. This solution follows immediately from the facts that, in *Figure 29*,

$$OM + ON + NH = OH = -p$$

and

$$OM \cdot ON = OC \cdot OA = q.$$

Graphical calculation can, however, be used not simply to find isolated values but also to find a whole set of values of a function $f(x)$ by measuring the ordinates of the curve $y = f(x)$ corresponding to values of the abscissa x. The curve is the equivalent of a single-entry table and, moreover, eliminates the need to interpolate between table values.

The curve is of course most easily constructed when $f(x)$ is a polynomial with integral powers, of the form

$$a_0 + a_1x + a_2x^2 + \cdots + a_nx^n.$$

J. A. von Segner explained how to construct[11] such a curve in 1761 and his method was rediscovered by Bellavitis[12] and has since been described by others, notably by Farid Boulad Bey, who has combined it ingeniously with certain principles of nomography.[13]

The need arises occasionally for the construction of what Professor R. Mehmke has called the *logarithmic image* of a polynomial, in which the abscissae and ordinates are proportional not to the values of the variable and the function but to their logarithms. Mr. Brauer has designed a special form of compasses for this purpose having three legs, of which the separations are related in a way determined by the definition of the "addition logarithms" of Leonelli and Gauss.[14]

2.2: Graphical Statics

Graphical methods are particularly well suited to the calculations required in problems of plane statics. The quantities to be operated on here are given directly as line segments, that is, in the form of vectors representing the forces whose equilibrium has to be studied. The three equations for the equilibrium of forces acting in the same plane can be expressed in a very simple geometrical form.

The *polygon of forces*, also called the *dynamical polygon* or Varignon's polygon, is the polygon formed by drawing a series of vectors having the same magnitudes, directions, and sense as the corresponding vectors representing the forces. The *funicular polygon* is formed by choosing an arbitrary point in the plane as a pole, joining this to each vertex of the force polygon, and then drawing lines parallel to these joins. The equilibrium conditions can be summarized by the statement

Both the force polygon and the funicular polygon, for any pole, must be closed.

The aim of graphical statics is to develop systematic methods, based on this principle, for the solution of any problem in plane statics. The methods that have been developed have, for a long time, been included in general technical practice.

Culmann[15] must be given the honor of being the first to put graphical statics into the form of a unified discipline in its own right, but several scientists and engineers before him had been concerned with applying the art of geometrical construction to the solution of such problems. To quote Mr. Favaro:[16]

> Poncelet made use of drawing to solve a large number of problems in mechanics. However, the majority of his constructions were not strictly graphical, but rather the translation into geometrical language of expressions previously found by means of analysis.... Before Culmann, Saint-Guilhem, Méry, and many others gave interesting graphical solutions to a variety of problems in statics that concerned the art of the engineer. Their studies, however, were limited to special questions and did not result in revealing general principles that could have formed a basis for general methods.

The first outlines of that body of knowledge on which the general methods of graphical statics were one day to be founded can be discerned in two important memoirs published by Lamé and Clapeyron when they were in the service of the Russian government[17] and even more clearly in a fine piece of work by Engineering Captain Michon,[18] then teaching at the École d'Application de Metz. Favaro commented that his teaching "... is entirely in the spirit of the methods of graphical statics, giving the first application of the properties of the force polygon and the funicular polygon to the stability of arches and fortifications."

Other studies were made in England by Taylor,[19] a draftsman with the construction company of J. B. Cochran, by Rankine,[20] and by Clerk Maxwell,[21] who even attacked the theory of reciprocal figures. But, once again, it was Culmann who, from 1860 onward in his lectures at the École Polytechnique in Zurich, succeeded in putting all the theories together to form a homogeneous whole.[22]

Several other people deserve mention as having significantly developed the foundations established by Culmann. These include: Cremona,[23] who showed the advantages that graphical statics can derive from the theory of reciprocal figures; Mohr, who by applying the method of the funicular polygon to elastic deformations opened the study of strengths of materials to new methods; Maurice Levy, who in his monumental work[24] generalized the methods to an extent never before suspected possible; and finally Rouché, who, by his teaching at the Conservatoire des Arts et Métiers, has contributed to the popularization of the new technique. It was Rouché who spread the technique to the construction companies, to whom it has been of immense value, and thus started the general dissemination of the techniques away from the preserve of engineers trained at the École de Zurich, where Culmann had laid the foundations.

As a final remark, we should mention that Professor B. Mayor of Lausanne, after a study of the very modern theory of linear complexes, has succeeded in developing a graphical statics of space.[25] This provides an elegant geometrical solution to problems of the equilibrium of forces that are not all in the same plane.

2.3: Graphical Integration

The aim of graphical integration is to construct *integral curves*, that is, curves representing either the integrals of functions that are themselves represented by curves and of which the integrals have therefore to be found by quadrature, or the integrals of differential equations.

The methods of graphical integration enable integrals to be found not only when the curve represents a function whose analytic form is known, but also when the function is only defined empirically. Because, in the latter form, the curve may represent the results of a series of experiments, the method is of the highest technical interest.

If the integral $\int y\,dx$ is regarded as the limit of the sum $\Sigma\, y\,\Delta x$ of very small quantities, it is obvious that the rigorous calculation of the integral can be replaced by a graphical calculation of the sum, using the method for summing the products of pairs of numbers that was explained at the start of this chapter. In order to ensure sufficient accuracy, the curve to be integrated must be broken into arcs that are short enough to be replaced by their chords without significant error. The value of y to be taken in each term is the ordinate of the midpoint of the chord.

In order to obtain an equivalent accuracy without having to take such small arcs, Massau has suggested replacing the arcs by cubic parabolas having the same tangents at the ends as the arcs they replace. This allows the arcs to have significantly greater curvature than in the case of replacement by chords and consequently reduces significantly the number required. It is possible to integrate the cubic parabola arcs by a simple geometric construction.[26]

Massau has also given a graphical solution for the problem of integration of first-order differential equations.[27] An equation such as

$$f(x, y, y') = 0$$

can be regarded as defining the direction of the tangent of the integral curve passing through the point (x, y) for each such point in the plane. Thus if we consider the curves along which y' has a constant value k, defined by the equation $f(x, y, k) = 0$ and called isoclines, we see that all the integral curves that cross the isocline corresponding to k have the same slope (k) at the point of intersection. We have introduced a device, which we have called the *directrix*, that greatly simplifies the tracing of these integral curves, constructing these as parabolic arcs joining points on the isoclines.[28] Important improvements to this method of graphical integration of differential equations have been made by Professor C. Runge.[29]

Graphical integration plays a major role in the study of the strength of loaded beams. In this application the variation along the beam of the shear force, bending moment, and the displacement of the neutral line are, respectively, the first, second, and fourth integrals of the load distribution.

The above-listed methods of obtaining graphical solutions are usually sufficient for most needs. More accurate drawings and results can be obtained by means of grapho-mechanical calculation, the subject of the next chapter.

Notes

1. ***10***. [(Ed.) References of this type refer to items noted in the bibliography at the end of this volume.]

2. ***22***.

3. ***20***.

4. ***25***.

5. ***24***.

6. ***5***, Chapter I.

7. *7*, Chapter IX, A.

8. ***5***, Numbers 13 and 14; *7*, Number 233.

9. *7*, Number 232.

10. ***5***, Number 18; *7*, Number 234. G. Arnoux also discovered this method independently and, moreover, devised an apparatus to reduce considerably the amount of trial and error involved in its use (*Bull. de la Soc. Math. de France*, Vol. 21, 1893, p. 93). The same method was also found by Commandant Deny (*Nouv. Ann. de Math.* 4th series, Vol. V. 1895, p 193).

11. ***5***, Numbers 19 and 20.

12. ***25***, p. 204.

13. ***5***, Number 75.

14. ***5***, Number 22.

15. (Ed.) See bibliography reference number 20.

16. ***25***, preface, pp. xxvi–xxix. However, it should not be forgotten that, even given the developments in graphical statics, purely geometrical solutions of problems in mechanics are not to be despised. [(Ed.) Collington, in particular, has proved many very elegant solutions.]

17. *Journal des Voies de Communication*, de Saint-Petersbourg, December 1826, p. 35, and January 1827, p. 43.

18. *Instruction sur la Stabilité des Voutes et des Murs de Revetement*, printed at Metz, November 1843, pp. 22, 24, 26. Culmann recognized very clearly Michon's claim to priority in this matter (see Preface to the French translation of ***20***, pp. ix–x).

19. According to a memoir of Professor Flemming Jenkin: "On the Practical Application of Reciprocal Figures to the Calculation of Strains on Framework," *Transactions of the R. Soc. of Edinburgh*, Vol. XXV.

20. *A Manual of Applied Mechanics*, London, 1872, pp. 115–124.

21. *Philosophical Magazine*, April 1864; also *Trans. of the R. Soc. of Edinburgh*, Vol. XXVI.

22. ***20***.

23. ***21***.

24. ***23***.

25. ***7***, Vol. II, Appendix 7. Since then Professor Mayor has greatly facilitated the study of his method by publishing his *Introduction à la Statique Graphique des Systemes de l'Espace* (Lausanne, 1926).

26. ***5***, Number 305; ***7*** Number 238. In this connection we have given a geometrical criterion for deciding when the approximation is adequate.

27. The graphical integration methods of Professor Saviotti, analogous to those of Massau, should also be mentiond; these were first published in *Giornale del Genio Civile* (Vol. XX, 1882, p. 172) and subsequently in *Revue Universelle des Mines* (2nd. Series, Vol. XIII, 1883, p. 483).

28. ***5***, Numbers 41 and 43; ***6*** Numbers 245 and 247.

29. ***27***.

Chapter III: Grapho-Mechanical Calculation

3.1: General Outline

Rather than performing one of the standard constructions for graphical calculation, it is often the case that one is able to use some piece of equipment whose operation duplicates the relationship between the various points that would have resulted from the construction. The use of this type of equipment is the essence of grapho-mechanical calculation.

Suppose, for example, that the intended construction involves only straight lines. It is clear that such a construction can be replaced by a set of straight rods linked in pairs by joints that can, if required, slide along the rods. Segner's method, mentioned above, for tracing high-order parabolas representing polynomials was transformed into such a set of rods by J. Rowing[1] in 1770, with the aim of solving algebraic equations by finding the points of intersection of the representative parabolas with the x axis.

Suppose, on the other hand, that a certain curve C has already been obtained, by using either Cartesian or polar coordinates, representing some function of a single variable; then a second curve C', representing another function of the same variable, can be derived from C by a geometrical transformation that can be performed by some suitable mechanical device. From this point of view the inverters of Peaucellier and Hart,[2] for example, can be regarded as instruments for grapho-mechanical calculation, as can the jointed rod devices made by Kemp[3] and by Mr. Roudaire-Miegeville[4] for tracing algebraic curves of arbitrary degree. An ingenious instrument consisting of a combination of two Peaucellier inverters was devised by the naval engineer Barrillon[5] for tracing the lines of hydrodynamical fields.

It is, in the field of integration, however, either definite or indefinite, that grapho-mechanical calculation has been of the greatest value. This aid has come about because of the development of the instruments called *integrometers*, for definite integration, and *integraphs*, for indefinite integration.[6]

3.2: Integrometers

Integrometers are a class of instruments that, as a result of the user following a closed contour with a tracing point fixed to the instrument, give the values of various integrals associated with the region enclosed by the contour, such as the area and the first moment and moment of inertia about a given axis.

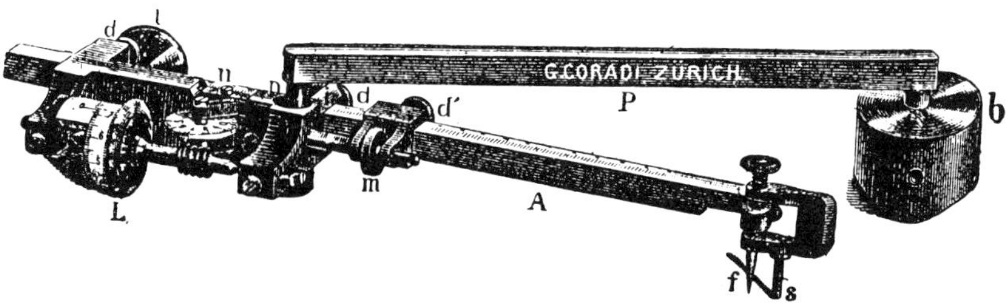

Figure 30

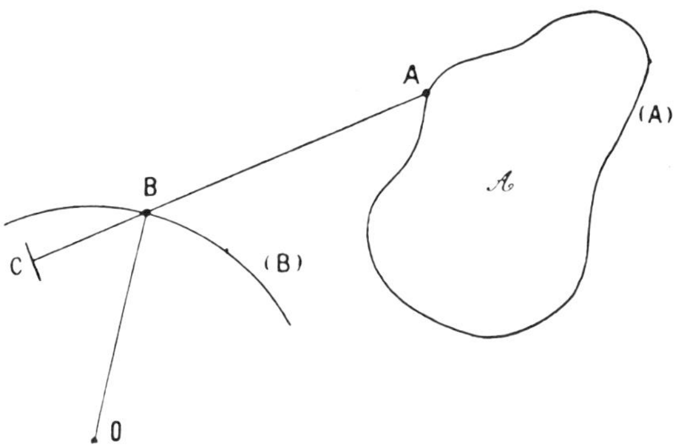

Figure 31

The simplest such instrument is the *planimeter*, which gives only the area enclosed by the contour. A Swiss engineer, Hoppikoffer[7] had the idea of an instrument of this type in 1827, but it was not until 1854 that his compatriot Amsler, with his discovery of the principle of the polar planimeter (*Figure 30*), gave the first truly practical solution to the problem of mechanical integration—a solution that has given rise to many variants since then.

The principle on which Amsler based his planimeter can be stated as follows:

1. In *Figure 31*, *AB* is a rigid rod of fixed length; if the point *A* moves round the contour (*A*) while the point *B* moves to and fro along an arbitrary curve (*B*), then the area enclosed by (*A*) is equal to the area swept out by *AB* as *A* makes a complete circuit of the contour.

2. *The area swept by AB* is proportional to the angle through which a wheel, whose axis remains parallel to *AB*, turns as it rolls without slipping on the plane of the paper.[8]

In Amsler's polar planimeter[9] the curve to which *B* is constrained is a circle, to the center, *O*, of which *B* is joined by a second rod *OB*. In Petersen's version of the device the wheel is replaced by a sleeve fixed to *AB* in a direction perpendicular to the rod and a simple device records the displacement of this sleeve in the direction of its axis, which is equivalent to the corresponding rotation of Amsler's wheel.

Other types of planimeters, called *rotation planimeters*, have been produced by Wetli, Richard, Amsler, and J. Thomson.[10] These are based on a principle first discovered by Hoppikoffer and involve the rolling of a wheel not on a plane but on the surface of a cone of which the generator passing through the point of contact is always parallel to the axis of the wheel.

If a system of planetary wheels is added so that the axis of the recording wheel no longer remains parallel to *AB*, but turns through either two or three times the angle turned through by *AB*, the recorded rotation gives the static moment or the moment of inertia, respectively, about an axis on which the point *B* is constrained to lie. This is the principle underlying the integrometer of Marcel Deprez, which is used for finding moments and moments of inertia.[11]

In Professor[12] Hele-Shaw's integrometer[13] the recording wheels or rollers do not rest directly on the paper but are driven by the rotation of spheres with which they are in contact.

Other integrometers have been designed for the purpose of giving the values of other definite integrals related to curves that the user must follow with the tracing point. Among these are the *harmonic analyzers*, which calculate, as definite integrals, the coefficients of the Fourier series representing phenomena resulting from the superposition of a number of periodic movements, as, for example, are met in the study of tides. The best known of these are the analyzers of Lord Kelvin, Henrici, Yule, Boucherot, and Sharp.[14] In addition to his analyzer, Kelvin constructed an instrument for performing the inverse operation of tracing the curve of the function expressed as a Fourier series, using the coefficients found by the analyzer. This distinguished mathematical physicist combined these two instruments, to form what he called the *tide predictor*,[15] in order to predict the rise and fall of the ocean tides. Clearly, if the height of the tide at a particular point on the coast has been recorded over a sufficiently long period of time, the use of the harmonic analyzer and tide predictor in succession will enable this to be predicted, for the same point, into the future.

The Dane Captain Prytz made the interesting observation that if as the end A of a rod AB makes a complete circuit of the periphery of an area S the end B is dragged along freely and so describes the tractrix curve of this contour, then the area S is approximately equal to the product of the length of AB and that of an arc of the circle, between the initial and final positions of B, whose center is the initial and therefore also the final position of A, and whose radius is AB. To apply this he provided the end A with a tracing point and B with a small knife so as to cut into the paper surface. He called this device a *hatchet planimeter*.[16]

By linking the hatchet planimeter to a particular system of jointed rods the naval artillery engineer General Jacob built a knife edge integrator capable of integrating differential equations of Riccati and Abel types. This device required that the tracing point follow a curve whose coordinates were found by simple quadrature operations on the given coefficients of the equations.[17]

3.3: Integraphs

Integraphs are the devices used when one wants to obtain not just a single value of one definite integral but the *integral curve* of a function, representing a series of indefinite integrals. The idea of such an instrument was first presented by Coriolis in 1836, in Liouville's *Journal de Mathématiques*.[18] The essence of Coriolis's idea was that a wheel, resting on the paper on which the integral curve was to be drawn, should be moved so that its plane was always in the direction given by the value of dy/dx at the point of contact, and that this wheel should be so firmly pressed into the paper that its instantaneous displacement would be in this direction. The idea was taken up by Zmurko in 1861 and exploited in an instrument described in *Cosmos* in 1884. Other forms have been proposed by other inventors, notably by Boys and by Mestre, but the instrument now used most widely for tracing continuous integral curves by means of simple quadrature is the one designed by the engineer Abdank-Abakanowitz, the details of which were later improved by the instrument builder Coradi (*Figure 32*). This instrument is based on the principle that (*Figure 33*) the tangent to the integral curve is always parallel to the line joining the point M_0 on the curve to be integrated (the tracing point) to a point P on the x axis whose distance from P_0, which is directly below M_0, is a constant. If, therefore, the direction of the axis of the wheel R is maintained perpendicular to M_0P, as

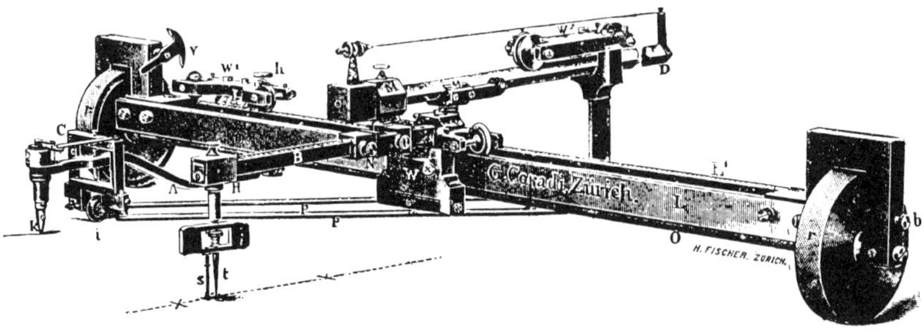

Figure 32

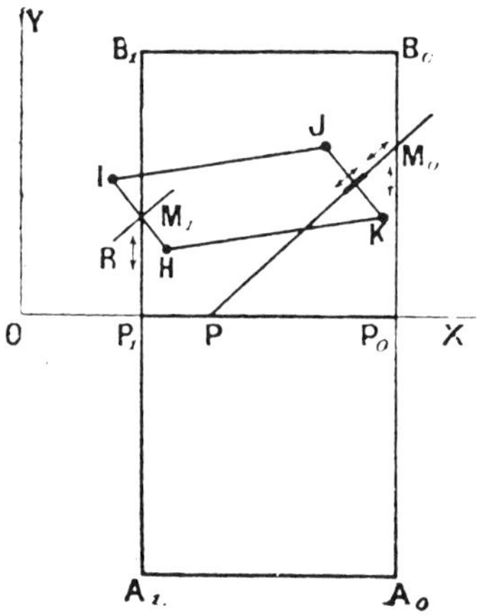

Figure 33

can be done by means of a freely jointed parallelogram, the instantaneous rotation of the wheel will always be in the required direction.

If what is required is not a simple quadrature but the integration of a first-order differential equation (of any form), then a more complicated method is needed for varying the direction of the tangent to the integral curve. However, in some cases, one might even say in all common cases, a curve related to the equation can be easily constructed such that, as this is followed by the tracing point, a relatively simple mechanical linkage enables the correct direction of the wheel axis to be found at each position of the tracing point.

Professor Ernesto Pascal of the University of Naples has devoted himself to the study of such integraphs. He has given careful accounts of the very remarkable results of his researches in an unusual book,[19] extracts from which we have included in our course at the École Polytechnique.[20]

Among the types of first-order differential equations that Professor Pascal has succeeded in integrating mechanically by this method are the Riccati equation, the linear equation in its most general form, and the equation of motion of a projectile in the air, the last of which merits special mention. It is well known that the main difficulty in the problem of experimental ballistics lies in finding an analytic expression for the variation of the air resistance with the speed of the projectile that is both close enough to reality and allows the equation to be integrated. The exceptional importance of Professor Pascal's grapho-mechanical method of solution is that while it uses the law of resistance obtained empirically, whose analytic form is therefore unknown, it enables the trajectory to be traced exactly for any given projectile. This shows very strikingly how the grapho-mechanical method can give practical results very simply that could only be obtained analytically with great difficulty.

Professor Pascal has also devised integraphs that operate with polar coordinates; the simplest of these is remarkably well adapted to the calculation of elliptic integrals of the first and second kinds, expressed in the standard form.[21] And, finally, he has shown how certain integraphs could be used to find numerical solutions to integral equations of the Volterra type.[22]

Professor Scatizzi of the Gregorian University of Rome has made important contributions to the study of integraphs;[23] and to Mr. A. Kriloff is due a type of integrator applicable to all ordinary differential equations, whatever their order or their form.[24]

Notes

1. *Lond. Trans.* Vol. LX, 1770, p. 240. According to Borgins (*Receuil Complet de Mécanique Appliquée aux Arts*, Vol. VIII, 1820, p. 226) a similar instrument had been designed previously by Clairaut.

2. *7*, Number 167.

3. *7*, Appendix, Note 6. Kemp has the honor of being the first to demonstrate the possibility of giving a mechanical construction for any algebraic curve whatever, but Roudarde-Miégeville's method is simpler.

4. *C.R.*, Vol. 176, 1923, p. 359; Vol. 181, 1925, p. 97.

5. *C.R.*, Vol. 182, 1926, p. 571.

6. For a detailled description of these instruments one should consult the book by H. de Morin, *Les Appareils d'Intégration* (Gauthier-Villars, 1913).

7. (Ed.) This name is spelled as Oppikoffer in the Napier Tercentenary Handbook.

8. *7*, Numbers 249 and 250.

9. *7*, Number 251.

10. For descriptions of these planimeters see ***29***, Chapter 1.

11. *7*, Number 253; ***29***, p. 107.

12. (Ed.) d'Ocagne had this name as Hell-Shaw in the original French version. The editors have corrected the spelling.

13. ***29***, p. 102.

14. ***29***, Chapter IV.

15. *7*, Number 164.

16. *7*, Number 252; ***39***, p. 42.

17. For the details see ***15***, pp. 370 and 383; also *7*, Appendix 8.

18. The different types of integraphs for quadratures can be found in ***29***, Chapter III.

19. ***30***.

20. *7*, Numbers 256 and 260. The examples given in this course were taken from ***30***.

21. *7*, Number 260.

22. *7*, Number 259.

23. *Nuovo Cimento*, issues of July 1914 and April-May-June 1921.

24. *Bull. de l'Acad. Imp. des Sc. de Saint-Petersbourg*, January 1904.

Chapter IV: Nomographic Calculation

4.1: General Outline

Suppose that we have an equation in several variables and that we set up a system in which various graphical elements, upon which we have marked graduated scales, are designed so that there is a simple graphical relationship, immediately perceived by the eye, between those graphical elements that represent a solution to the equation. We shall then have produced a graphical representation of the equation with which, if we are given the values of all but one of the variables, we can find the remaining value by simply reading it from one of the graduated scales. This construction gives us, in some sense, an *image of the algebraic mathematical law expressed by the equation*, which we may describe by the name *nomogram*, which is a combination of the two Greek words for *law* and *I draw.*[1]

In general, nomograms can consist of systems in which the graduated scales are either fixed or are movable with respect to each other. In this case the rules for numerical calculation, being divorced from their ultimate physical meaning, can be regarded as nomograms in their own right.

This rather indefinite concept, which we shall make more precise later, already shows that nomograms can be regarded as tables of completed calculations. Their graphical form, however, gives them inestimable advantages over ordinary numerical tables: great reduction in the time needed for their construction, much less space occupied, and great ease of visual interpolation. One must, of course, recognize that nomograms of normal size are limited to an accuracy of only a few figures, usually three or four, while tables can be taken to whatever degree of accuracy is required.

When there is a need for a larger number of significant figures, as in astronomical or financial calculations, nomograms can be used only to give a first approximation, an operation that is often of value. These fields apart, however, there are vast areas of application in which the degree of approximation given by nomograms is broadly sufficient, notably in several branches of engineering science. There is no need to labor this point; the facts are sufficiently well known to have long ago provided the proof of what is claimed here.

There are, however, two particular considerations that show the decisive superiority of nomograms over tables. The first is that, as we shall show later, they allow the number of variables to be easily increased, almost without limit. The second is that they allow us to evaluate implicit functions just as easily as explicit functions. We may say that when we represent an equation by a nomogram it is the very construction of the nomogram that solves the equation: this concept will be made much clearer in later examples, after which we shall return to its discussion in greater detail. The type of difficulty encountered in tabulating an implicit function is readily appreciated when one sees that, for any set of given values, the value of the unknown can be found only by an indirect, and sometimes lengthy, procedure.

From this last point of view the importance of nomograms is truly fundamental and they are seen as one of the most valuable mathematical tools.

Before embarking on a summary of the different types of nomograms now in common use, it is necessary that we give a short sketch of their historical development.

4.1.1: A Glance at the History of Nomography

It is very interesting to note that the first indication of the concepts that were one day to be joined together in this body of knowledge can be detected in a number of instruments designed in the Middle Ages. These instruments were generally created with the needs of various astronomical calculations in view, a typical example being the *quadratum horarium generale* described in the 15th century by Regiomontanus in his *Calendarium*.[2] On the other hand it was the logarithmic scale of Gunter,[3] the invention of which goes back to the 17th century, in which we first have the representation of a function by a graduated scale. It was finally the geometry of Descartes that established the possibility of representing any function by means of a geometric curve.

It was not until the appearance, in 1797, of Pouchet's book *Arithmétique Linéaire*[4] in Rouen that the first attempt at the systematic construction of graphical tables with two entries is found. It was this that prepared the way for the methods of nomography.[5] Pouchet's tables are strictly two-entry ordinary Cartesian graphs, which will be described later, and earlier examples of such tables can be found that were used for certain special calculations.[6] Pouchet was, however, well aware of the scope of the method he introduced, as can be seen from the following extracts from his book:[7] "The advantage of graphical calculation[8] is that it provides the possibility of working quickly and without any need for pen, paper, or ink, because it provides, in a sense, a universal table of calculations that have already been made.... This linear arithmetic may become as universal as ordinary calculation."

Despite their authority, we cannot agree with Lalanne and Favaro[9] when they express their regret that Pouchet did not see that his *lignes d'égal élément* represented projections on to the plane of the paper of sections, parallel to this plane, of certain surfaces. Had he done so it would have enabled him to identify immediately, as Terquem did later,[10] ordinary two-entry graphs as a means of representing topographical surfaces.[11] Clearly, Terquem's observation helps to give a simple geometrical form to the principle on which these special nomograms are based, but no great benefit can be derived from this because the method cannot be extended to more general nomograms. For these we need to consider, as Pouchet did, only systems of graduated lines in the plane and not trouble ourselves with relating these to geometrical entities external to the plane.

Several later authors also used this method for graphical representation of formulae with two variables, foremost among them being d'Obenheim,[12] an officer in the Génie Militaire and professor at the École de Strasbourg; Bellencontre,[13] from the Artillery; Allix,[14] an engineering officer in the Marines; and Davaine, an engineer in the Ponts et Chaussées.

In 1842 Léon Lalanne, also an engineer in the Ponts et Chaussées, proposed the use of graphical tables of this type for calculating the profiles of various earthworks. This appeared in an appendix to the *Résumé du Cours de Construction* by Sganzin. In 1843 he formulated the now classic principle of *anamorphosis*,[15] which, by reducing many of the curves to straight lines, greatly encouraged the development of these two-entry graphical tables, or *abacs* to use Lalanne's term.

As we shall see later on, the principle underlying anamorphosis, which had first been expressed by Lalanne for a particular case, was not given in its general form until 1884. This generalization was done by Massau, who was an engineer in the Belgian Ponts et Chaussées and also a professor at the University of Ghent.[16]

We ourselves, in 1884, introduced a much more fundamental reform into the field of graphical representation by considering only points as labeled elements instead of straight lines. This had consequences of major importance, leading, in 1891, to the development of a method of great generality,[17] which gave a *direct* representation of equations of more than three variables in those cases where the equation cannot be separated into sets of equations of only three variables. It is for this reason that the method of aligned points can be said to have made possible, for the first time, the *effective* reduction of a four-dimensional geometrical entity to a plane representation. Despite this advance, the technique of separating an equation of many variables into sets of equations, although it does not give a direct representation in the case of more than three variables, is of undeniable practical importance and was used systematically, if still in a rather special form, by Mr. Lallemand from 1885 onward in connection with his *hexagonal graphs*. In the case of equations of three variables, Lallemand's hexagonal graphs are really the anamorphosed graphs of Lalanne, the difference being only in Lallemand's more practical layout.

It was the coming together of all these different methods, different in appearance and starting from quite different origins, that gave the present author the idea of amalgamating them into one unified account by showing how they can be derived systematically from a single starting point.[18] This, then, was the origin of *nomography*. This body of knowledge, outlined for the first time in 1891,[19] was completely presented in the *Traité* published in 1899.[20] Chapter IV of that work concluded with the development of the most general morphological theory, encompassing all the *possible* modes of nomographic representation. It is this theory that will form the underlying theme in the following account. The classification to which it first led us has, since then, been simplified in our later publications.[21] It can be said that the treatise of 1899 definitively established the autonomy of nomographic calculation within the general field of graphical calculation.[22] Before the appearance of that volume the first vestiges of the subject had been there, but only in a scattered form.

Nomography not only synthesizes a homogeneous unity from a number of specialized procedures, but it also allows different specialized procedures to be developed in an orderly way by adapting them to deal with any new requirements that may arise. This systematization also eases the burden on those who are attempting to learn the procedures for the first time because it provides a framework upon which to build detailed levels of knowledge. As an introduction, the work by Mr. Gercevanoff[23] makes clear the good account to which nomography can be put in graphical and graphomechanical calculation.[24]

After this short historical sketch of nomographic calculation we shall give a few indications of its most commonly used principles. During this presentation we shall draw, in the most general way, upon the abovementioned theory of the structure of nomograms.

4.1.2: The General Form of Nomograms

In a nomogram a correspondence is established between the continuous set of values, within given limits, which can be taken by a variable z, and a system of geometrical elements (points or lines), which is defined in terms of a parameter taken equal to z, each element being labeled with the corresponding value of z. Of course, only elements corresponding to the discontinuously increasing values of z (usually to values in an arithmetic progression) can be shown; those corresponding to intermediate values are located mentally between these by what is called *visual interpolation*.

If the labeled elements are points, they form what is called a *scale*. These points can lie on any geometrical structure whatever. If this structure is a straight line and if the distance (as measured from the origin) along this line to the point labeled z is proportional to a function $f(z)$, we have a *scale for this function*. The commonest scales are metric, logarithmic, and trigonometric (sines, tangents, or their logarithms). The scales needed in practice can generally be derived from these by simple processes.

If what is required is a system of labeled lines,[25] we can say, without going into details, that these can be found by constructing the scales formed by the intersections of these lines with various transversals and joining identically labeled points with continuous lines. This is the method used to construct diagrams in descriptive geometry, in which the lines of intersection of surfaces are determined point by point.

In general, doubly labeled lines (that is, lines depending on two parameters) and, *a fortiori*, lines with more than two labels, cannot be shown on the diagram; but a system of *doubly labeled points* can be envisaged. These will appear as the nodes of a *network* formed by the intersections of two families of lines, each singly labeled, one by z_1 and the other by z_2, the point (z_1, z_2) being common to the line (z_1) of one family and the line (z_2) of the other.

As indicated above, the form of every nomogram is the expression of a *graphical relation* between labeled elements taken from various systems displayed together in the diagram. But what do we mean by a graphical relation? We can easily convince ourselves that the only kind of graphical relation that can be judged, with sufficient precision, by eye is that of intersection, or *graphical contact*, either between two lines or between a line and a point. The latter includes the case of parallel lines, which is equivalent to the contact between one line and the point at infinity on the other.

It is very rare, however, that we need to consider contacts between lines, and consequently in a work like this we can limit ourselves to contacts between points and lines.[26] This means that every form of graphical relation leading to nomograms of this type will reduce to the observation of simultaneous contacts between points and lines. It is also worth remarking that the coinciding of two points is equivalent to two contacts, of one of the points with each of any two lines running through the other; one can also regard it as being of three contacts, of one of the points with three lines running through the other.

We must also point out that any possibility of contact between a singly labeled line and a doubly labeled point brings the possibility of representing an equation in three variables. If the graphical relation being planned depends on n such contacts simultaneously, the corresponding equation can involve $3n$ variables.

The foregoing is the basis of the *morphological* theory of nomograms mentioned previously. We shall not go into this in any more detail, but shall draw on it in the following descriptions.

The theory just sketched enables us to classify all the possible types of nomograms.[27] If we are concerned only with their form, then from the time this theory was first formulated it became impossible to *invent* any new types. If, however, we view them from their use in various applications, we must recognize that a special theory must be developed for each type of nomogram in order for it to be usable in practice. This theory must cover the determination of the canonical form of the corresponding equations, the conditions under which a given equation can be reduced to this form, the means by which the simplest way to perform this reduction can be found, the simplest way to construct the nomogram, and what form it should take in order to be most useful. These are all questions that raise important mathematical problems of greater or lesser difficulty and give scope for considerable skills of invention and ingenuity. It is in work in these areas that several writers have made contributions of importance to nomography. The most notable of these are Farid Boulad,[28] Clark,[29] Gercevanoff,[30] Goedseels,[31] Lallemand,[32] Margoulis,[33] and Soreau.[34]

4.2: Concurrent Line Nomograms

4.2.1: Cartesian Graphs

The simplest case is that in which the use of the nomogram is limited to establishing a single contact. If this contact is between a singly numbered

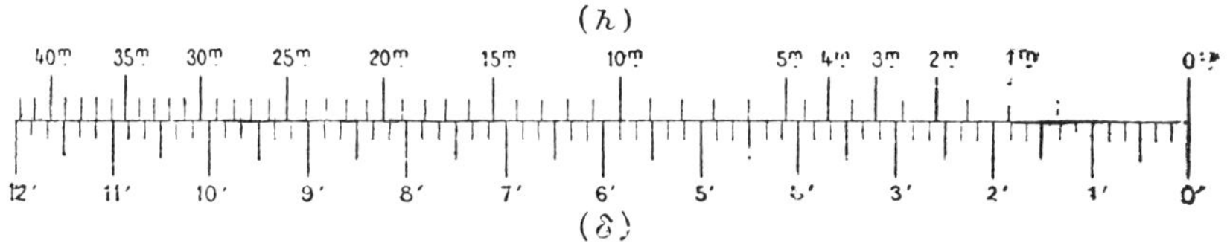

Figure 34

line and a singly numbered point, or between an unnumbered line (i.e., a *constant line*) and a doubly numbered point, we have two alternative methods for the representation of equations in two variables. In one method, the singly numbered points can always be taken on a straight line and the singly numbered lines perpendicular to this line; further, the numbers attached to these latter lines can be written at their intersections with the axis of the first scale and the representation is thus reduced to the writing of the two scales on the two sides of a single axis as in *Figure 34*. This nomogram gives the depression, δ, of the horizon as a function of the observer above the surface of the sea.

In the other method, the doubly numbered points can always be defined by means of a regular grid composed of two sets of parallel lines, each numbered with values of one of the variables, the constant line representing, in Cartesian coordinates, the given equation. This is the usual graphical method, which is universally employed to display the relationship between two variables and is familiar even to those who are strangers to mathematics. *Figure 35* shows the application of this method to Gauss's law giving the number of errors per 1000 for which the ratio to the probable error is given by p.[35]

If we now take the contact to be between singly numbered lines and doubly numbered points, we have a method of representation that can be applied to any equation in three variables. In each case we can, as was done above, define the network of doubly numbered points by means of a regular grid. It is then possible to produce the Cartesian representation of an equation in three variables, of which *Figure 36* is one of the first examples (actually the nomographic multiplication table of Pouchet), the use of which has also become universal. The chessboard appearance of the network has led Lalanne to call such a drawing an *abacus*.[36]

In short, with such a nomogram the graphical relation is given by the intersection (concurrency) of three numbered lines, each carrying a value of

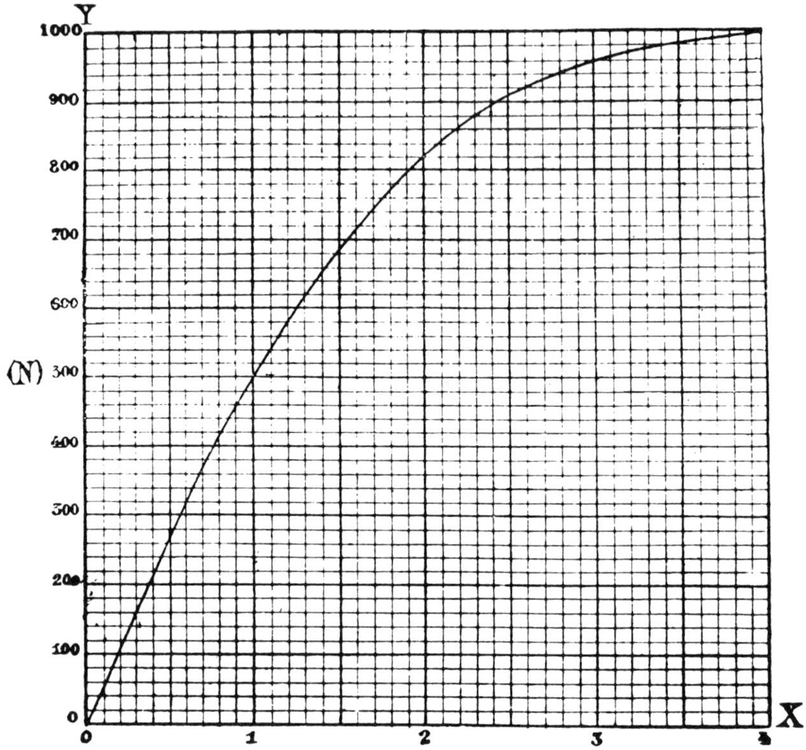

Figure 35

one of the variables in question. Thus such a nomogram can be characterized by saying that it is of the *concurrent line* type. As the use of the regular grid applies to all cases of equations in three variables it would seem unnecessary to consider other forms of representation for such equations. We shall, however, see that certain variations of form can offer a number of advantages.

4.2.2: Anamorphosed Graphs

Lalanne in 1842[37] was the first to point out that if the axes of the grid were drawn through points (on the X and Y axes) spaced not on a metric scale but on some functional scale (in particular, on a logarithmic scale) then certain advantages would result. In some cases the curves representing the third variable, the drawing of which could be a long and tedious process, could be replaced by straight lines.

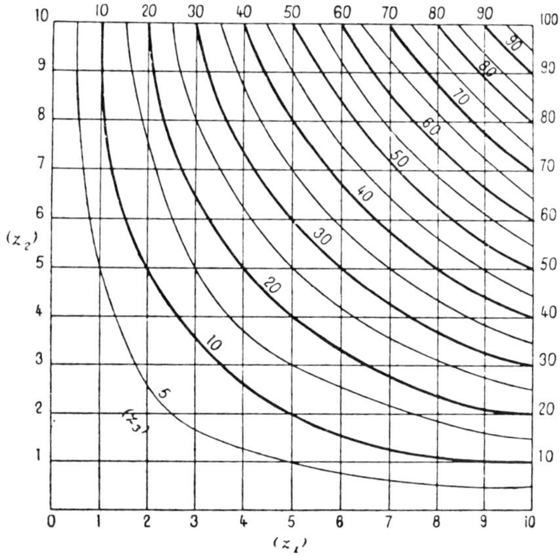

Figure 36

In particular the equation for multiplication,

$$z_1 z_2 = z_3,$$

if put into the form

$$\log(z_1) + \log(z_2) = \log(z_3),$$

gives the graph of *Figure 37*, equivalent to that of Pouchet (*Figure 36*) in which the curves are rectangular hyperbolae. Such a translation has been given the name *anamorphous* by Lalanne. We may say that the graph of *Figure 37* is an anamorphosism of that of *Figure 36*. There are many cases in practice in which the use of an irregular grid brings about the same simplification.[38]

Lalanne's anamorphosism reduces to substituting an irregular grid, in which the spacing of the axes depends on certain functions, for the original regular grid. In cases where the simple Lalanne anamorphosis will not suffice to convert the representation of the third variable into a system of straight lines, we can change the representation of the first two variables from lines parallel to the axes to any system of lines whatever (*Figure 38*).

This deeper transformation, first considered by Massau,[39] depends on a

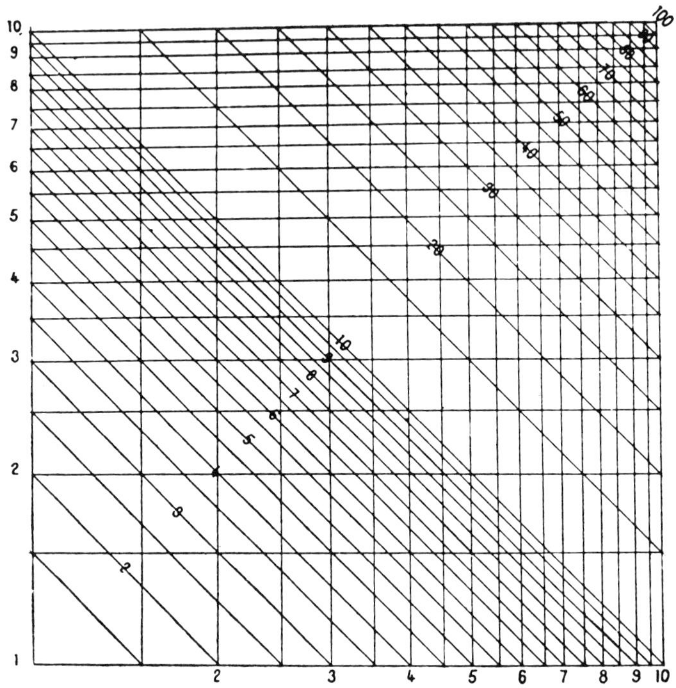

Figure 37

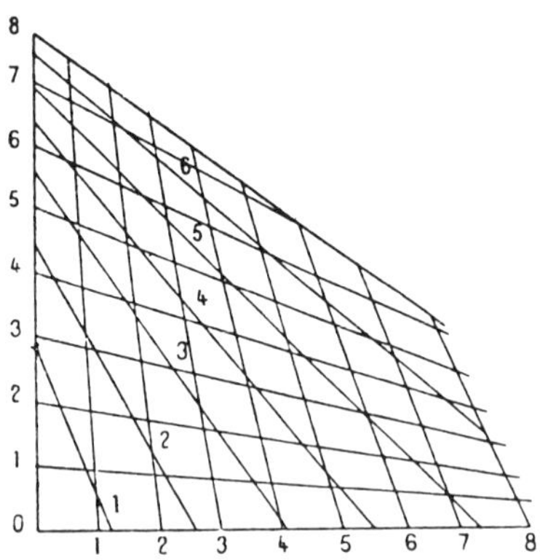

Figure 38

mathematical theory that goes beyond the limits of the present work. However, the point to be noted is that the great majority of equations in three variables can be represented by this transformation in three systems of concurrent straight lines. Among the few for which this is not the case it is found that a simplified representation will result from using circles, which are also easy to draw. This gives rise to what is known as *circular anamorphosism*, the straight line form being called a *rectilinear anamorphosism*.

It should be noted that while it is only natural to use straight lines to represent the first two variables in the equation, there is no mathematical necessity for this, and, in fact, the choice of these two representational systems is purely arbitrary. We, for our part, have given a complete theory of circular anamorphosism.[40]

4.2.3: Hexagonal Graphs[41]

Let us now pause for a moment to examine the case in which the simple anamorphosism gives a system of numbered parallel straight lines for each of the three variables. In this case we denote by f_i a function of the variable z_i, so that the equation to be represented has the form

$$f_1 + f_2 = f_3.$$

In such a case, it is possible to write the numbers for the lines forming each system on an axis perpendicular to the common direction of the lines, and place over the plane of the drawing a transparency on which there are three concurrent index lines (I_1, I_2, and I_3) parallel to the directions of the three axes. If this transparency is given any translation displacement whatever (therefore keeping the same orientation), then the graduations of the points in which the indexes meet the axes will always be the values of the variables z_1, z_2, z_3 that satisfy the equation (*Figure 39*).[42] Several writers have had the idea of such a device,[43] but it was Mr. Lallemand who took it to a very happy conclusion by changing the disposition of the axes so that these make angles of 60 degrees with each other (*Figure 40*) while still setting the index lines perpendicular to these scales. In the original form, if the scales on the X and Y axes are f_1 and f_2, respectively, that on the T axis is $f_3/\sqrt{2}$, whereas in this second form the three scales are f_1, f_2, and f_3 uniformly.

Since, as before, each scale can be displaced perpendicular to its direction, while maintaining this direction, the layout of *Figure 41* can be

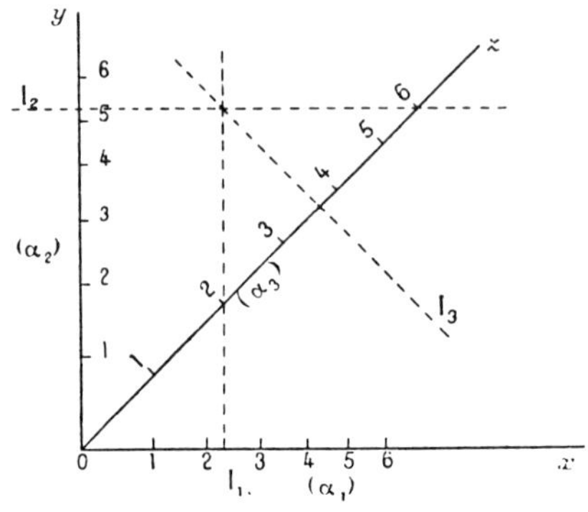

Figure 39

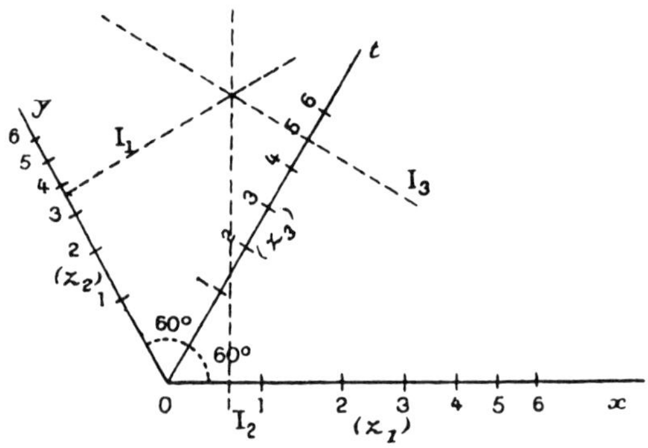

Figure 40

achieved. Here the scales f_1, f_2, f_3 lie on the sides of an equilateral triangle and the indexes are the diagonals of a movable regular hexagon—hence the name *hexagonal graph* used by Mr. Lalanne for this form.[44]

4.2.4: Partitioned Graphs for Equations in Several Variables

In general, the method of concurrent lines cannot be used to represent equations in four or more variables. With four variables it is necessary to establish contact between doubly numbered points and lines that are numbered not singly but doubly. It is not, in general, possible to show a doubly infinite system of lines on a single plane—hence the impossibility stated above.

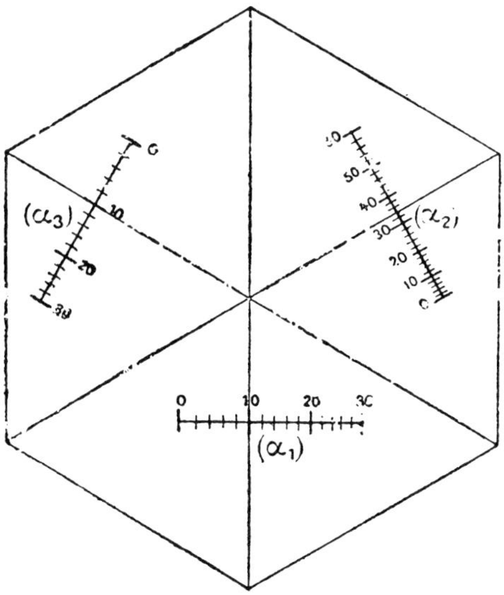

Figure 41

There is an exception to this impossibility only when the lines of the system can be reduced to a single line of infinite length. Each such line then corresponds to an infinity of pairs of numbers, and as it therefore appears as the condensation into a single line of a single infinity of doubly numbered lines, it may be called a *doubly numbered condensed line*.

Consider, for example, a graph for an equation in the three variables z_1, z_2, ξ in which the lines (ξ) are the perpendiculars to the X axis through the points of the metric scale for ξ marked on this axis. To each pair of values of z_1 and z_2 there corresponds a line (ξ) passing through the intersections of the lines (z_1) and (z_2). Each (ξ) line thus corresponds to an infinity of pairs of values of z_1 and z_2 and is therefore a condensed line numbered by z_1 and z_2.

If we now make these same lines (ξ) form part of the graph for an equation in ξ, z_3, and z_4, we have, as a result of the linking of the two graphs by the common system (ξ), a representation of the equation in four variables obtained by eliminating ξ between the two equations represented by, respectively, the two partial graphs thus linked. This shows that the four variable equation in question must be of the form

$$f(z_1, z_2) = \xi, \qquad g(z_3, z_4) = \xi,$$

which are then linked by the common system (ξ). In other words, *the representation of such an equation in four variables is obtained by partitioning it into two nomograms, each of three variables, by means of the auxiliary variable ξ.*

The system of lines (ξ) forms what Mr. Lallemand has called a *binary scale*, in z_1 and z_2 on the one hand, and z_3 and z_4 on the other. Thus the method just described for the representation of an equation in four variables of this form can be defined as the simple linking of two binary scales, just as the first method given here for the representation of equations in two variables results from the linking of two single scales.

It will be seen that whenever single scales on straight line axes are involved, the number of variables can be doubled by replacing these single scales by binary scales on the respective axes.

This is just what Mr. Lallemand has done in his hexagonal graphs. It was he, in conjunction with Eugene Prévot, who made the first systematic use of binary scales, although other writers had used them in special cases apparently without appreciating their general usefulness. *Figure 42* is a

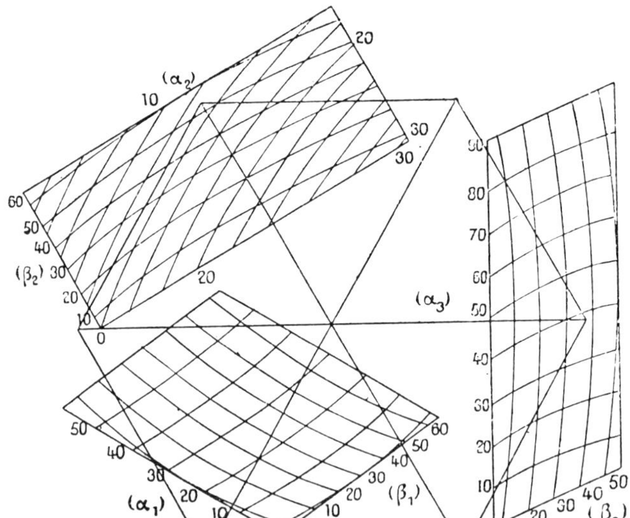

Figure 42

schematic diagram of a hexagonal graph in six variables, representing an equation of the form

$$f(z_1, z_2) + f(z_3, z_4) + f(z_5, z_6) = 0.$$

It will be seen that such a graph separates into four partial nomograms representing the equations:[45]

$$f(z_1, z_2) = \xi_1, \qquad g(z_3, z_4) = \xi_3, \qquad h(z_5, z_6) = \xi_5,$$

$$\xi_1 + \xi_3 + \xi_5 = 0.$$

It is clear that in the same way each of the two systems of singly numbered lines used to define a system of doubly numbered lines can be replaced by a system of doubly numbered condensed lines, defined in its turn by the confluence of two singly numbered systems, and so on. *Figure 43* shows a system C of quadruply numbered condensed lines.

By successive applications of this process, equations in any number of variables can be represented. The representation consists of linking a number of nomograms, each of only three variables, which resulted from partitioning the original equation into a set of equations in three variables. The system of equations will require the use of auxiliary variables, and these will correspond to a system of lines whose purpose is simply to establish the required relations between the systems numbered with the values of the variables in the original equation.

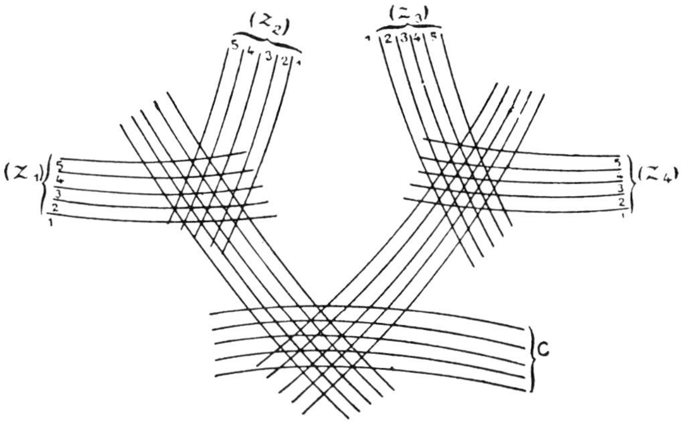

Figure 43

It is not always possible, however, to find a separation of a given equation into a set of equations in three variables. In practice it is often found that equations in four variables can not be reduced to the form[46]

$$f(z_1, z_2) = g(z_3, z_4),$$

one of the simplest examples being the complete equation of the third degree:

$$z^3 + nz^2 + pz + q = 0.$$

Thus there is a need for a direct method of representation of equations in more than three variables that does not involve partitioning. Such a representation may be called *intrinsic* for the number of variables in the equation considered. We shall see (and this is one of the most important features of nomography) how such an intrinsic representation can be obtained by basing it on the principle of collinear points rather than on that of concurrent lines.

4.3: Collinear Point Nomograms

The method of collinear points, which was first published by ourselves,[47] developed from the observation that the lines forming a concurrent line nomogram are often confusing. The eye can wander when trying to follow a line to the point where its number is written, and this means that interpolation by eye is rather uncertain. This is very obvious in the example shown in *Figure 44* (which has not been constructed for this purpose but comes from a graph made recently by Mr. Théry of the École Forestière to aid in survey work). The X and Y axes of the regular grid are graduated with numbers representing the data, and the lines are drawn representing the values of the result of the computation. The values of the result are written on the Y axis and coincide with the values of the Y axis. Any attempt to use this nomogram will make the difficulties just described only too obvious.

As the great majority of equations in three variables that are encountered in practical applications can be represented by systems of concurrent straight lines, using some anamorphism if necessary, it occurred to us that all of these difficulties could be abolished. It is possible, by means of a dual transformation, to replace lines by points, thus resulting in a nomogram in which points on a single straight line correspond to a situation in a

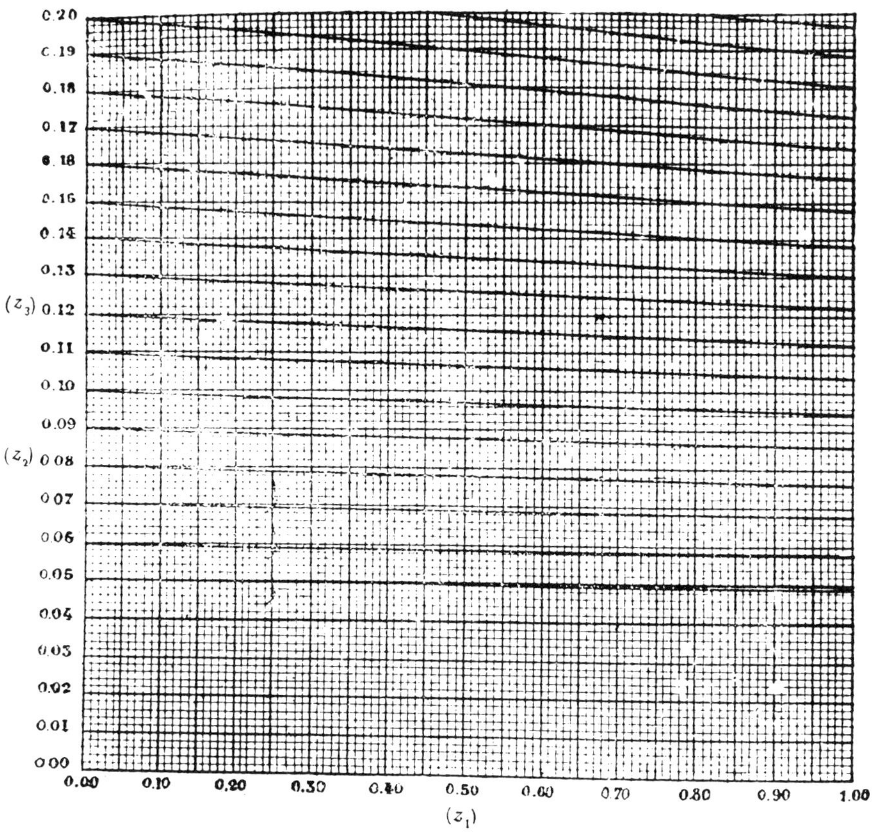

Figure 44

concurrent line system where straight lines meet at a point. With this transformation there would no longer be any confusion in reading because each number would be attached to only one point, and interpolation by eye would be much easier because it would need to be done between points on scales instead of within systems of lines.

There are, as will be shown, additional advantages to this form of nomogram. However, there is also one disadvantage: the classical dual transformation, that of reciprocal polars, would replace the Cartesian coordinates used for concurrent line nomograms by Plücker coordinates, and these, unlike Cartesian coordinates, do not represent segments of lines but rather the inverse of such segments. This gives rise to no difficulty as

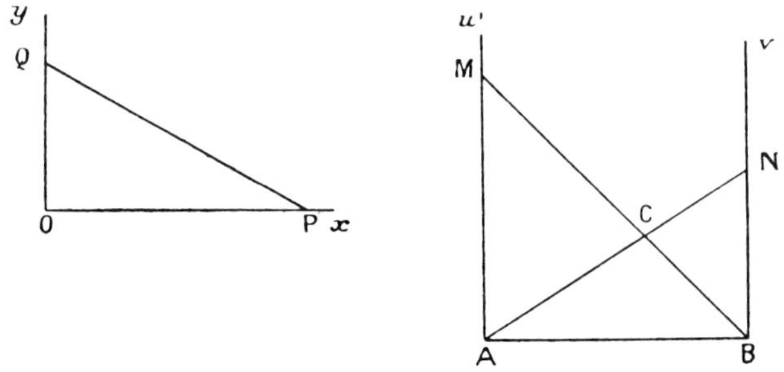

Figure 45

long as they are used for theoretical subjects (such as proof construction) but leads to serious complications when what is required is a graphical construction for practical use. This consideration led us to look for a system of tangential coordinates that would, like the Cartesian system, give simple line segments.

Our study led us to define a system of what we have called *parallel*[48] coordinates as follows. *Au* and *Bv* are axes through the origins *A* and *B*, respectively. The parallel coordinates of any line in the plane are the segments it makes on these axes, measured from the respective origins and, of course, taken with respect to sign. Thus to the points

$p\ (x = a, y = o)$ and $Q\ (x = 0, y = b)$,

referred to on the Cartesian axes x and y, there correspond the lines

$BM\ (u = a, v = 0)$ and $AN\ (u = 0, v = b)$,

referred to on the parallel axes *Au* and *Bv*. Thus the point *C* is transformed into the line *PQ* (see *Figure 45*).

When applied to the graph of *Figure 44*, this transformation gives the nomogram of *Figure 46*. A simple comparison of these two nomograms shows very clearly the advantages claimed above for the method of collinear points. In fact another advantage also becomes immediately clear: while it is impossible in *Figure 44* to decide whether or not the lines of the third system all pass through a single point—something one must know if one wishes to derive the equation from the nomogram (which was derived in this instance from experimental results[49])—the doubt is removed in *Figure 46* since the points of the third system lie on a curve (a conic) and not

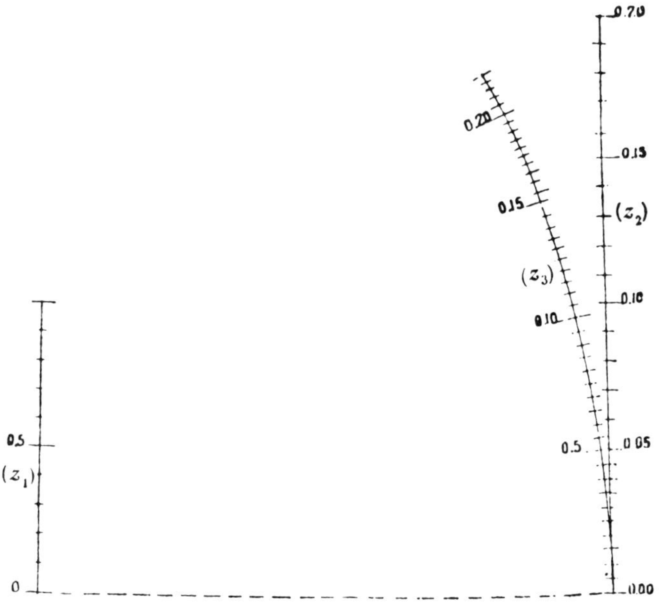

Figure 46

on a straight line. This implies that the lines of the third system cannot be concurrent.

So far we have confined ourselves to showing how, as a consequence of their origin, collinear points are related to concurrent lines. However, it is, of course, possible to construct this new type of nomogram directly.

In the course of constructing a collinear point nomogram it is often the case that purely geometrical considerations enter, often unexpectedly,[50] into the process to give the result a much simpler form than the corresponding concurrent line nomogram. Without stressing this subject further, which is treated in detail in our main writings,[51] we may note two points where the geometry gives particularly interesting results. For the first, we have shown how the general homographic transformation (the importance of which had up to now been regarded as purely theoretical) enables such a nomogram to be given, *a priori*, the layout most convenient for practical use.[52] For the second point, we have made clear the importance of the role played by what we have called the *critical values* of the variables of the equation[53] in the projective construction of the scales in the corresponding

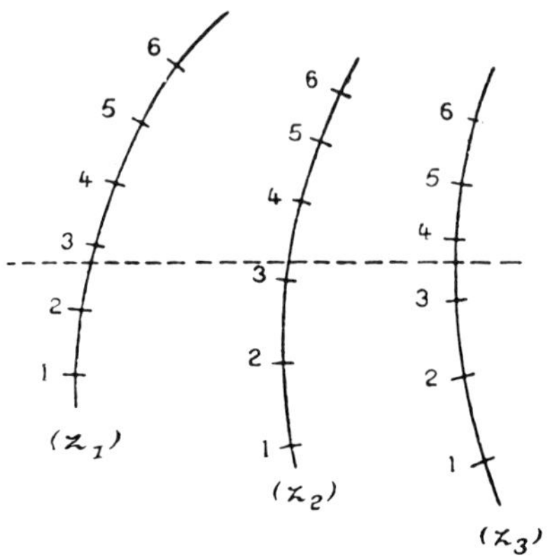

Figure 47

nomogram. On this last point, Mr. F. Boulad has given some interesting generalizations of our method.[54]

The three scales in a collinear point nomogram may be curvilinear.[55] If they are, the type of nomogram formed corresponds to one of three systems of concurrent straight lines that has resulted from a rectilinear anamorphism of the most general kind considered by Massau[56] (see *Figure 47*).

Whatever the nature of the scales, the graphical relation reduces in all cases to having the index line[57] make a single intersection or contact with each of the three scales. There is, however, nothing preventing us from replacing these singly numbered points (on the three scales) by the doubly numbered points of a network. Thus we have the possibility of doubling the number of variables without any partitioning of the nomogram and of thus obtaining *intrinsic* representations of equations in four, five, or six variables.

The method of collinear points thus brings a new advantage, of major importance, compared with that of concurrent lines. The majority of equations found in practical applications, while not amenable to the partitioning required for the use of condensed lines, can be represented by the method of collinear points. It will suffice to show in detail the treatment of the complete equation of the third degree mentioned earlier,

$$z^3 + nz^2 + pz + q = 0,$$

for which the method of collinear points gives a nomogram (*Figure 48*) that

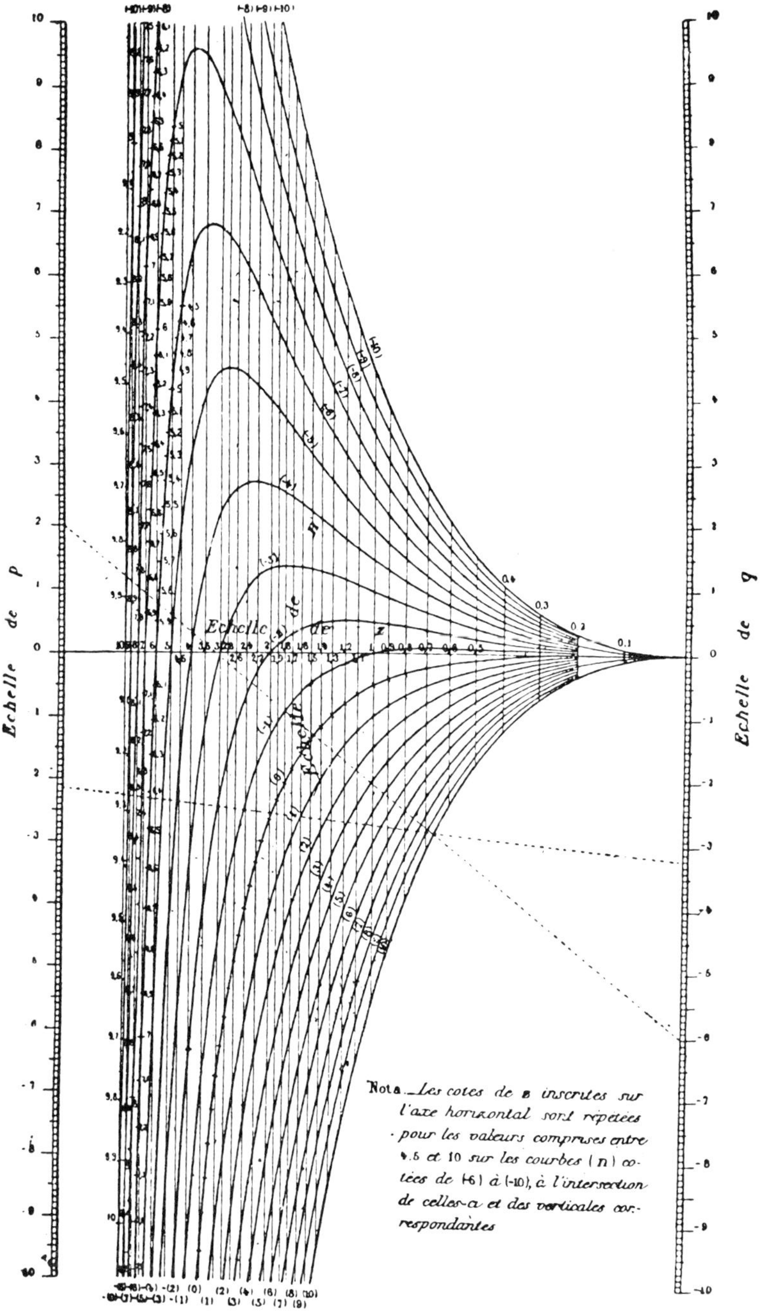
Echelle de p
Echelle de q
Echelle de z
Echelle de n
Nota. Les cotes de z inscrites sur l'axe horizontal sont répétées pour les valeurs comprises entre 4.5 et 10 sur les courbes (n) cotées de (-6) à (-10), à l'intersection de celles-ci et des verticales correspondantes

Figure 48

is very easy to use and for which the construction is purely geometrical and remarkably simple.[58]

In this nomogram the two parallel straight line scales correspond to the variables p and q respectively; a system of numbered curves corresponds to the variable n; and a system of lines parallel to the first two scales corresponds to z. Thus, if the values of n, p, and q are given, all that needs to be done in order to solve the equation is to stretch a line between the points p and q on the corresponding scales and to read the numbers on the parallels passing through the points where this line meets the curve numbered n.[59]

The dotted index lines shown in *Figure 48* correspond to the two equations

$$z^3 + 2z - 6 = 0 \qquad \text{and} \qquad z^3 + z^2 - 2.16z - 3.2 = 0,$$

for which one finds

$$z = 1.46 \qquad \text{and} \qquad z = 1.6.$$

This example brings out, to some extent, the advantage mentioned earlier of nomograms over calculation when the quantity required is defined implicitly, rather than explicitly, in terms of the data, as in this case, where z is defined as a function of n, p, and q. Apart from the fact that it is not possible to make a single numerical table having the three entries n, p, and q, if the values of z had to be determined for all values of these three variables between certain limits, it would entail laborious calculations for each such set of values.

The situation is entirely different with the nomogram. The scales (p) and (q), the parallels (z), and the system of curves (n) are all constructed *separately*, and entirely independently of one another, by the simplest of geometrical procedures. It is then the simple action of placing the index on the drawing that, by establishing the graphical relation between the elements numbered with the given values of n, p, q, and z, *solves* the equation at the moment when the solution is required.

Several important extensions have been made in the method of collinear points, in a variety of directions, notably by the method of *movable parallels* due to Mr. Beghin,[60] by the *arbitrary transversals* of Mr. Goedseels,[61] by the method of *equidistant points* of Mr. Gercevanoff[62] (for the case where the index is a circle), and finally, and above all, by the methods of *double* or even *multiple alignment*, which we ourselves have proposed.[63] This last extension has been taken up and developed by Mr. Soreau in his writings,[64] where he gives some very interesting applications.[65]

The method of collinear points has shown itself to be so fruitful in practice that Mr. Goedseels has said that it is in this method that the essence of nomography resides.[66]

It goes without saying that we ourselves have made so many nomograms for practical application, sometimes in response to requests from various technical specialists, that it would not be possible to list them all here. They can, however, be grouped into three general areas, the details of which can be found in our main treatise.[67] These three are problems in the calcualation of cross sections of embankments and cuttings, the general solution of spherical triangles (to meet the needs of astronomy and geodesy), and the construction of artillery firing tables.

This last application was made in the office for nomographic studies that we supervised as part of the Direction des Inventions during the last two years of the war.[68] Many other applications of the nomographic method were made during the war in order to meet various technical needs that were important to military operations. In particular, a whole harvest of applications came from the technical aeronautics section, concerning the construction and use of airplanes. Another important application was in connection with the manufacture of heavy artillery in the Schneider factories; laborious calculations required for the design of reinforcing windings for gun barrels were reduced by Mr. L. Potin to a few collinear point nomograms. Engineer-General Jacob, of the naval artillery, has also provided nomograms of this type for the solution of all the standard problems of exterior ballistics.

The best demonstration of the practical value of the method is provided by the innumerable applications made by writers, of all nationalities, to a very wide range of special problems. Many of these writers have been willing to share their nomograms, and we have collected them together at the École des Ponts et Chaussées. This collection is of such size and breadth that the catalogue alone, which today contains over 500 entries, would fill a complete booklet.

A number of these nomograms are for individual formulae; others fall into groups dealing with several different special techniques. It will suffice here to draw attention, apart from the varied collections made by Mr. Soreau and Mr. Seco, which encompass several branches of engineering science, to the publications of Mr. Aubry (on reinforced concrete), Engineer-Colonel Bertrand (water flows), Farid Boulad Bey (bridge design calculations of all types), J. Eichorn (properties of gases), Mr. Gorrieri (bridge design calculations), Mr. Kraitchik (financial calculations), naval artillery Engineer-General Jacob (exterior ballistics), Lieutenant-Colonel Lafay (siege guns), Russian Artillery Colonel Langensheld (coastal mortar firing), Spanish Artillery General Ollero (ballistics), Commandant Millot (statistics), Merchant Navy Captain Perret (navigation), Mr. Pesci (naval movements), Mr. Potin (railways, reinforcing windings of gun barrels), Mr. Poussin (insurance), R. Proell (steam turbines), Italian Frigate Captain Ronca (firing of naval guns), Mr. Seefehlner (electric railways), Mr. Stevez (hydraulics), Mr. Vaës (machine construction), Mr. Wolff (irrigation of Egypt),[69] etc.

The practical advantages of the collinear point method are such that Lieutenant-Colonel Lafay has proposed that it be used to solve *any* equation in three variables, at least approximately and within certain limits. The graphical method that he has devised for this purpose[70] is of the greatest ingenuity and has already been of great practical value.

Finally, it should be noted that this method has proved remarkably effective in revealing the analytic form of certain physical laws derived from experimental data. In this context we may quote the researches of Commandant Batailler on the air resistance of projectiles, of Mr. Beghin on the formula for the tractive effort of a locomotive of a given type, of Lieutenant-Colonel Lafay on the initial velocity of projectiles, of Mr. Rateau on the theoretical efficiency of steam engines,[71] etc. However, one of the most remarkable applications of the method in the experimental sciences is surely that made by Professor L. J. Henderson of Harvard University in the study of respiratory phenomena in blood.[72] While this book was being printed we received from Professor Erik J. Warburg of Copenhagen an interesting collinear point "haematological" nomogram intended for use in certain biological studies.[73]

4.4: Nomograms with Movable Scales

With collinear point nomograms the contacts that constitute the graphical relationship are between numbered points, whose positions are fixed, and an index line. The index line can be considered as a constant (i.e., unnumbered) element that is movable over the plane of the nomogram. This naturally gives rise to the idea of increasing the number of variables that can be represented, while preserving the intrinsic nature of the representation, by replacing the movable constant element by movable numbered elements.

In general, the position of a movable plane π' with respect to a fixed plane π depends on three parameters. This position is determined by establishing three contacts between elements of the two planes—for example, three lines of π' with three points of π. Once the relative position of the two planes has been fixed, we can consider the contact of a fourth line of π' with a fourth point of π. In this case we shall have produced a type of nomogram in which the graphical relationship consists in the simultaneity of four contacts. Because each of these contacts can be established by means of a singly numbered line and a doubly numbered point, without any partitioning (a process peculiar to condensed elements, for which the multiplicity of numbering can be increased indefinitely), this provides a means for constructing nomograms for the intrinsic representation of equations in up to twelve variables.

The first statement of this principle in its general form is to be found in a note by us to the Académie des Sciences, in 1893.[74] All of the previously described methods involving a movable constant element (hexagonal graphs, collinear point nomograms, etc.) now appear as special cases of this general principle. Similarly, some of the much older instruments produced to simplify calculation, such as the calculating rules dealt with in Chapter V, are reduced to special cases of this general principle.

If two of the four simultaneous contacts are fixed as the coincidence of the axes Ox of π and $O'x'$ of π', the two remaining contacts can be established between the lines of two distinct systems of parallels to $O'x'$ in π' and the points of two graduated scales parallel to Ox in π. This gives a design for a type of nomogram that is not practical because of the difficulty of its construction.

The case in which one of the four contacts is between $O'x'$ and the point at infinity on Ox (i.e., the two axes are parallel) can be considered separately. In this case the plane π' is of *fixed orientation*. The elements entering into the remaining three contacts can then be chosen freely, so that if each is between a doubly numbered point and a singly numbered line, an intrinsic representation of an equation in nine variables has been made possible. A deep study of nomograms of this type has been made by Mr. Margoulis, former director of the Eiffel aerodynamics laboratory, who has called them *oriented-transparency nomograms*.[75] He has published a large number of very remarkable applications of the technique, mainly in the areas of aerodynamics and aviation.

Professor R. Mehmke had previously published an ingenious nomographic method for the solution of certain equations[76] that, *a posteriori*, is seen to belong to this general type with the inclusion of the principle of logarithmic anamorphism due to Lalanne. Mehmke gives the name *logarithmic image* of a function $f(z)$ to the curve representing this function for which the Cartesian coordinates (for each value of z) are $x = \log z$, $y = \log f(z)$. In this system, all the images of an algebraic trinomial in z can be generated by the movement of a single curve drawn on the oriented plane π' and, similarly, all the images of a quadrinomial by the movement of a system of singly numbered curves in this oriented plane. It follows that Mr. Mehmke's logarithmic image nomograms can be applied to the solution of algebraic equations having up to six terms, and therefore, in particular, to all complete equations of up to and including the fifth degree.

By increasing the number of movable planes applied one above the other, with three contacts to fix the position of each with respect to the initial fixed plane, representations can be produced that are still intrinsic and that apply to indefinitely increasing numbers of variables.[77] This is the situation in calculating rulers having several slides and also of Hansson's rulers.[78]

This short account will doubtless suffice to demonstrate the possibilities offered by nomography, which are, in a sense, unlimited.

Notes

1. The name *nomogram* was first used in the title to the book ***2***.

2. Further details can be found in "La Calcul Nomographique avant la Nomographie" in *Annales de la Société Scientifique de Bruxelles*, Volume XLVI, 1926, p. 55.

3. (Ed.) Edmund Gunter, Professor of Astronomy at Gresham College in London, 1619–1626.

4. ***31***.

5. In the second edition of the book *Échelles Graphiques des Nouveaux Poids Mesures et Monnaies de la Republique Francaise*. In the first edition the charts had to be read with the aid of compasses, but this was no longer necessary in the second edition, where the charts had, in effect, become nomograms.

6. Notably the Longitude Tables and Horary Tables constructed by Margetts, published in London in 1791. Mr. P. Luckey, in his interesting study *Zur Aeltern Geschichte der Nomographie*, published in 1923, has shown that similar examples can be found in the earliest Greek and Arabic scientific work; in this connection he quotes the Analemma of Ptolemy.

7. Reproduced by Mr. Favaro in the preface to his *Leçons de Statique Graphique* (Volume 1, page 20).

8. What is being discussed here is what we have called Nomographic Calculation in this book.

9. Loc. cit., p. 21.

10. In *Mémorial de l'Artillerie*, 1838; his observations related to Bellencontre's graphical tables, described later. There is another note by Terquem in the same volume, on Obenheim's tables.

11. According to Mr. Favaro (***25***, p. 154) the use of level curves, which has been known since the 16th century (*Astronomique Discours*, Jacques Bassantin, 1557) and was familiar to the Dutch in the 17th century (*Art du Fontainier*, P. Jean-Francois, 2nd, edition 1665, p. 25), was suggested as a method for representing the relief of the Earth's surface by Philippe Buache (*Mémoires de l'Académie des Sciences*, 1752), by Ducarla (*Expression des Nivellements*, 1782), and by Dapain-Triel (*Méthode Nouvelle de Nivellement*, 1804). The same graphical representation was used for other physical quantities, as, for example, by Halley in the 17th century for the magnetic declination. It led to the isotherm lines of Humbolt (1813), and since then to a host of analogous curves, among which isobars published every day by the Bureau Central Météorologique are especially well known.

A final remark is that this method for representing the results of experiments involving two variable quantities was used by Piobert in 1825 (*Mémorial de l'Artillerie*, Vol. I, 1826) and has long been standard practice among technical workers. See, for example, Professor Marey's *La Méthode Graphique dans les Sciences Expérimentales* (Paris, Masson, 1878).

12. *Balistique*, 1814. Also *Mémoire Contenant la Théorie, la Description et l'Usage de la Planchette du Canonnier*, 1818.

13. *Mémorial de l'Artillerie*, 1830. This concerns the graphical representation of Lombard's tables and is what led Terquem to the observation referred to in the previous paragraph.

14. *Explication d'un Nouveau Système de Tarifs*, 1840.

15. *C.R.*, 2nd series, 1843, p. 492. This subject is developed further in ***32***. So far as the use of this method for calculating earthwork profiles is concerned, Lalanne improved the layout of the charts considerably (ibid., 1st series, 1850) by using an ingenious idea due to Davaine and applied by the latter in certain anamorphosed tables of his own (*Mémoires de la Société des Sciences de Lille*, 1845). Lalanne himself gave a very full account of his methods in the volume of Notices published by the Ministère des Travaux Publics on the occasion of the Exposition Universale of 1878 (pp. 429–484). It is clear from this that the work on the same subject done in Germany and published by Herrman (1875), Helmert (1876), and Vogler (1877) and in Holland by Kapteyn (1876) added nothing essential to Lalanne's method.

16. ***24***, Book III, Chapter III, 2.

17. ***1***. The method is developed under the name *méthode des points isoplèthes* in Chapters IV and VI of our 1891 publication, and taken to its full development in Chapters III and V of our *Traité*, where it is given the name used here.

We take this opportunity to comment that if the solutions to certain particular problems given previously by various authors, notably by Möbius (*Journal de Crelle*, Vol. 22, p. 280) and by Kutter and Ganguillet (Oestr. Ing. und Arch. Ver. Zeitschr., Vol. XXI, p. 50) could be expressed in terms of the method of collinear points, analogously to the expression of Mercator's transformation in terms of the principle of anamorphosis, these would do nothing to make clear the general principles on which systematic applications of the method could be based. Our mémoir *Le Calcul Nomographique avant la Nomographie* (*Ann, de la Soc. Scien. de Bruxelles*, Vol. XLVI, 1926, p. 55) may be consulted for further details.

18. There is an ambiguous statement in the preface to our publication ***2*** (p. 4) that, if taken to apply to graphs in general rather than only to the hexagonal graphs mentioned in an earlier paragraph, may give the impression that it was the theory of the latter that provided the starting point for our own work. We wish to make it clear that our research, published in 1884, was entirely independent of that of Mr. Lallemand, who did not publish his work until 1886; and that it was only later that we developed the subject systematically and included the work of Lallemand and Massau.

19. ***2***.

20. ***3***.

21. ***4*** and ***5***.

22. In this connection we should like to call on the authority of Mr. Maurice Levy, the main proponent of graphical statics in France, who has written as follows (*G.C.*, Vol. XXXV, p. 425): "To replace the multitudinous variety of numerical scientific calculations, whenever graphical representation will give the required degree of approximation, by graphs from which the required results can be read at a glance—such is the aim of a *new chapter in science* deserving *to be ranked with* descriptive geometry and graphical statics, which Mr. Maurice d'Ocagne .... has developed into a discipline to which he proposes to give the name of *nomography*" (the italics are ours).

23. ***37***.

24. Summaries of nomography, all drawing to a greater or less extent on the account that we have given, have been published in many languages—in particular: in German by F. Schilling (Leipzig, 1900), P. Luckey (Berlin, 1918), F. Krauss (Berlin, 1922), B. M. Konorsky (Berlin, 1923), O. Laemann (Berlin, 1923), K. Schwerdt (Berlin, 1924); in English by P. de Beaurepaire (Madras, 1907), C. Runge (New York, 1912), R. K. Hezlet (Woolwich, 1913), J. Peddle (London, 1910, 2nd edition 1919), Brodetzky (Leeds, 1920), J. Lipka (New York, 1921), Henz and Sewarp (New York, 1926), A. Esnouf (Port Louis, Mauritius, 1926); in Arabic by F. Boulad-Bey (Cairo, 1908); in Japanese by K. Ogura (Tokyo, 1923); in Spanish by R. Seco de la Garza (Madrid, 1910), L. Guttierez del Arroyo (Madrid, 1914); in Dutch by F. J. Vaës (Rotterdam, 1902); in Italian by G. Pesci (Livourne, 1901), G. Ricci (Rome, 1901); in Polish by W. Laska (Lemberg, 1904), F. Ulkowski (Lemberg, 1905); in Rumanian by J. Jonesco (Bucarest, 1900); in Russian by N. Gercevanoff (St. Petersburg, 1906); etc.

25. (Ed.) "Lines" is intended, in the general sense, to include curves.

26. (Ed.) Most people using nomograms tend to think of the process as finding intersections of lines; however, the process is really one of finding which lines intersect different grid points. The grid points are themselves usually represented by intersecting lines, and this tends to add some confusion to the difference between a point and a line.

27. ***3***, Numbers 147–149; ***5***, Numbers 100–103; ***10*** Numbers 23, 24.

28. A resumé of the principle contributions of Mr. Boulad in this area are the subject of Appendix II in ***3***.

29. ***37***.

30. ***38***.

31. ***34***.

32. ***33***.

33. *C.R.*, Part One, 1922, p. 1684. Mr. Marhoulis is preparing a report on his nomographic research.

34. ***35*** and ***36***.

35. (Ed.) ρ is not marked in this graph! it is the X axis.

36. Despite the very well defined etymology of this term we had chosen to extend its use (both in our first publications on the subject and in our major treatise of 1899) to all tables presented graphically, of whatever type. While many writers have been happy to use the term in this general sense we have subsequently felt it more correct to adopt the name *nomogram*, first proposed by Professor Schilling. [(Ed.) It is likely that the term *abacus* was adopted because of the grid's superficial resemblance to the standard European table abacus, which, in turn, gave its name to a number of gridlike patterns.]

37. See Note 15.

38. It is relevant here to draw attention to a most remarkable fact: very many physical laws relating two experimentally determined variables are represented by straight lines on such a logarithmic grid. The English physicist C. V. Boys, whose work is famous for the remarkable ingenuity displayed, told us during a visit to his laboratory in London in May 1896 that he had found this to be so common that he now always, as a first step, plotted his results on logarithmically ruled paper. A very typical example is the work done by Mr. Rateau (*3*, No. 90) leading to the law of consumption of a steam engine. Logarithmic paper is now available commercially.

39. ***24***, Book III, Part 2, Chapter III. It will be shown later (Note 56) that we ourselves conceived the general idea of anamorphosis at very much the same time without having the slightest knowledge of Massau's work.

40. ***3***, Numbers 46, 47; ***5***, Numbers 54, 55.

41. The theory of hexagonal graphs is given in ***3*** (Chapter II, Section III, and Chapter III, Section II).

42. It is clear that each of the three scales can be given an arbitrary displacement in the direction of its index, the direction of the scales remaining constant.

43. In particular, Mr. Blum in connection with Mr. Lalanne's profiles for embankments and cuttings (*A.P.C.*, 1st series, 1881, p. 455).

44. Because of the relative positions of the scales, which is an essential feature of this method of representation, the term *equilateral graph* would perhaps have been preferable.

45. If one of the first three of these four equations—say, for example, the first—is linear in the variables z_1, z_2 that enter into it, then this also can be represented by a hexagonal graph, for which the axis of ξ_1 is the same as the corresponding axis of the fourth equation and the axes of z_1 and z_2 are parallel to those of ξ_2 and ξ_3. The two hexagonal graphs are thus partially contiguous and the same transparency can serve for both; it is then possible to move from one to the other by simply sliding the transparency in the direction of the index line perpendicular to the common ξ_1 scale, which otherwise would not need to be shown on the drawing. Thus it is seen that the ingenious idea of sliding the transparency, due to Mr. Lallemand, corresponds precisely, from a theoretical point of view, to that of binary scales.

46. The necessary and sufficient analytic conditions for this reduction to be possible are given by Mr. Goursat in *Bull. de la Soc. Math. de France*, Volume XXVII, 1899, p. 27.

47. ***1***.

48. *7* (Number 11) contains a general theory of dual tangential coordinates, leading to the idea of these particular coordinates. It was shortly after conceiving this idea, the complete theory of which we gave in *Nouv. Ann. de Math.*, 1884, that we realized that such coordinates had been evisaged by Chasles in 1829 (see Quetelet's *Corr. Math.*).

49. See, for example, Mr. Rateau's research on the theoretical consumption of steam engines, in ***3*** (Number 90) and ***5*** (Number 74).

50. Remark made by J. Tannery in the *Bull. des Sc. Math.* (1899, p. 175).

51. ***3***, Chapter IV; ***5***, Chapter IV.

52. ***3***, Numbers 63, 86; ***5***, Number 62.

53. ***3***, Numbers 74–76; ***5***, Numbers 68–70; ***10***, Number 15.

54. ***3***, Appendix III.

55. The analytical criterion for deciding whether a given equation can be reduced to the canonical form required by this method of representation was given by Mr. R. N. Gronwall (*Journ.* de Math. Pures et Appl., 6th series, Vol. VIII, 1912, p. 59).

56. It was by this route that we ourselves, completely unaware of Massau's work, were led to the idea of this general anamorphosis.

57. A fine line traced on a transparency by means of a taut thread.

58. ***3***, Number 104; ***5***, Number 73.

59. The nomogram constructed in this way gives only the positive roots of the equation; the absolute values of the *negative* roots are the positive roots of the equation obtained by changing z to $-z$, which results from changing n to $-n$ and q to $-q$, keeping p unchanged.

60. ***3***, Numbers 125, 126.

61. ***34*** and ***3***, Numbers 128, 129.

62. ***3***, Number 132; ***5***, Number 92.

63. ***3***, Chapter V, Section II; ***4***, p. 54.

64. ***35*** and ***36***. In ***38*** J. Clarke of the École Polytechnique de Caire gives the first practical examples of the application of the method of double alignment to the case of a *curved line of pivots*. His paper contains developments of the greatest interest concerning equations that can be represented by collinear point nomograms with *scales of degree higher than one*.

65. Here we may note Mr. Mehmke's suggested extension of the method of collinear points in space (*coplanar points*), of which he has given an ingenious application (***3***, Number 109); Mr. Soreau has commented (***36***, Number 91) that the method of double alignment can be derived from this as a special case. Finally, we may mention a type of nomogram due to Mr. Furle, in which the index is a deformable polygonal line (*Sitzunbsber. de Berliner Math. Gesellsch.*, 1903, p. 26).

66. Many of the accounts of nomography quoted earlier limit themselves to a description of this method.

67. ***3***, Chapter V, Section III.

68. See ***8***. The corrections to the firing conditions required to take account of variations in atmospheric conditions (pressure, temperature, wind speed, and direction) were given by our nomograms in less than 2 minutes, whereas calculation would have required 15 to 20 minutes.

69. See ***3***, pp. xii and xiii.

70. *G.C.*, Volume XL, 1902, p. 298.

71. See ***3***, Numbers 88, 89, 90; ***5*** Numbers 74, 80.

72. *C.R.*, Volume 180, 1925, p. 2066.

73. (Ed.) This sentence originally appeared as a "Note Additionelle" printed on a separate page between the Bibliography and the Index. It was accompanied with the notation that the reference to Warburg's work should be placed "immediately after the important work of Professor Henderson." The editors decided to include it in its intended place rather than print it as a separate note at the end of the book.

74. *C.R.*, Volume 117, p. 216 and 277.

75. *C.R.*, Volume 174, 1922, p. 1684. See also, in the same volume, our note on p. 1664.

76. *Zeitschr. f. Math. u. Phys.*, Volume 35, 1890, p. 174. See ***3***, Numbers 139, 140, 141; ***5***, Number 98.

77. ***3***, Number 146; ***6***, Number 101.

78. ***5***, Number 95.

Chapter V: Nomo-Mechanical Calculation

5.1: Logarithmic Instruments

If some of the geometrical coincidences that are required in the use of a nomogram are brought about by some physical device, we say that the arrangement constitutes a *nomo-mechanical instrument.*[1] Examples of this type of device are rulers that can slide, or disks that can turn, with respect to each other, but the term is not used for more complex devices, which would more properly be called mechanisms or machines.

The most important instruments of this type are those whose scales are logarithmic and are therefore called *logarithmic instruments.* The concept of logarithm, on which the function of these instruments is based, can very easily be explained to those who have little mathematical knowledge: all that needs to be said is that algebra provides us with a method that, given any number N, gives a related number, called the logarithm of N, which is written $\log N$, such that if N is the product of two numbers N_1 and N_2, then $\log N$ is the sum of $\log N_1$ and $\log N_2$. Thus the use of logarithms reduces multiplication and division to addition and subtraction.[2]

5.1.1: Instruments with an Index: Rulers, Circles, Helixes

Very soon after Napier's wonderful invention of logarithms, efforts were made to simplify their use by applying the same principle to the representation of numbers on a graduated scale. The underlying idea is very simple and, to us with out present mathematical education, seems quite natural; however, if we cast our minds back to the time at which it was conceived, we cannot fail to admire the profound wisdom of the man to whom the honor of this is due, the Englishman Edmund Gunter (1581–1626), who published it in 1624.[3]

Gunter's idea was to mark, on a straight line, points whose distances from a fixed origin are proportional to the logarithms of successive numbers, writing against each mark the number whose logarithm it represents (*Figure 49*). An axis graduated in this way is called a logarithmic scale; originating in the early 17th century, it is the first example of a functional scale, a concept that has been generalized and used extensively in nomography.

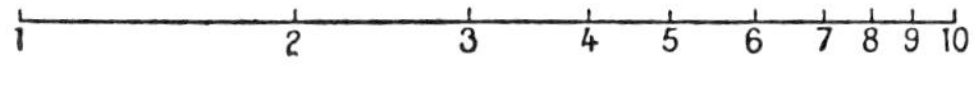

Figure 49

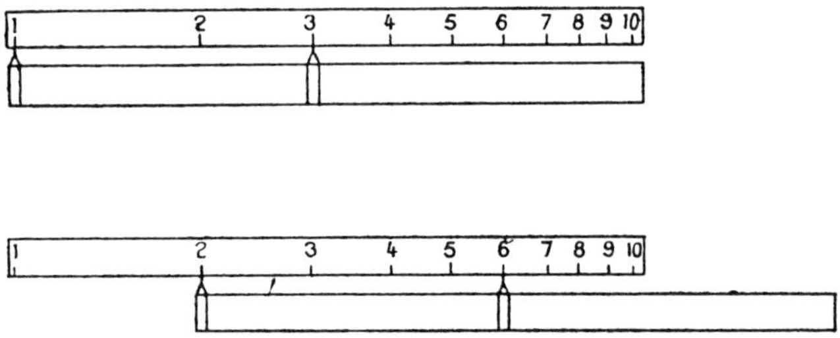

Figure 50

How can such a scale be used to multiply together two numbers, A and B? A compass, or a pair of dividers, is opened by an amount equal to the distance between the point marked 1 and the point marked B. It is then moved along the scale so that one leg of the compass is at the point marked A, and the other leg will then be at the point marked with the value of $A \cdot B$. The reason this works is that the distance between the two points of the compass is $\log B$. That same distance is then measured off, starting at the point $\log A$, so that the second leg of the compass is now at the point $\log A + \log B$, which is the point $\log(A \cdot B)$.

Instead of using the compass to add the logarithmic segments we can mark the scale on a ruler and place a second, identically marked, ruler along side the first. By sliding the second ruler along the first we can substitute the scale markings for the points of the compass. This is shown in *Figure 50*, which illustrates the example of 2 times 3.

The edge along which the two scales meet can also be curved in the form of a circle or helix. This is because these two curves share, with a straight line, the property that they can be made to coincide at all points along their length. The circle and helix do, however, have the advantage over the straight line in that they allow a greater length of scale to be contained in a more compact device: the longer the scale, the greater the number of digits that can be represented in each number.

In the case of the circular form of this device the graduated circle and the movable index must be able to turn independently of each other about the center. In the other form, the graduated helix with a ring index, the movable index must be capable of both sliding along the length of the helix and rotating in the plane of the ring. There must also be the possibility of relative movement between the two indexes and the graduated scale, but any one of the three elements can be assumed to be fixed in place. For

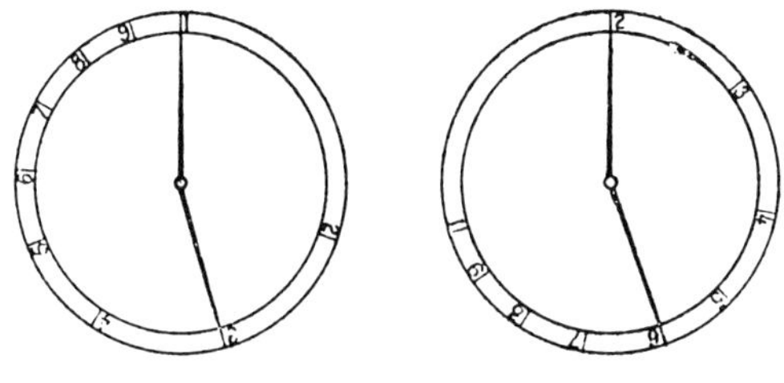

Figure 51

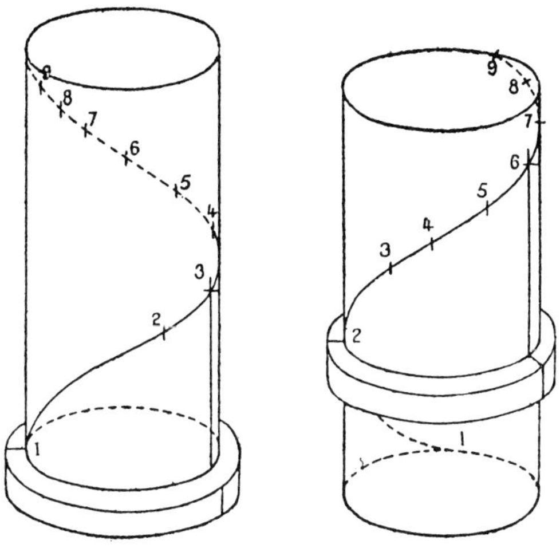

Figure 52

example, in the case of the circle, the circular graduation can be kept fixed and the two indexes made movable but linked so that the movement of one entrains movement of the other with the angular separation of the two remaining constant; it must also be possible to set this angular separation at any desired value. *Figures 51 and 52* illustrate the methods of using the circle and helix scales, again using the example of 2 times 3.

According to Mr. Favaro, whose important historical research has cast a most revealing light on the origins of logarithmic instruments, the first circular scale was made by Oughtred[4] in 1632 and the first helix by Milburn[5] in 1650. These forms of logarithmic scales can be found on many modern instruments. For example, in Boucher's arithmetical dial[6] (*Figure*

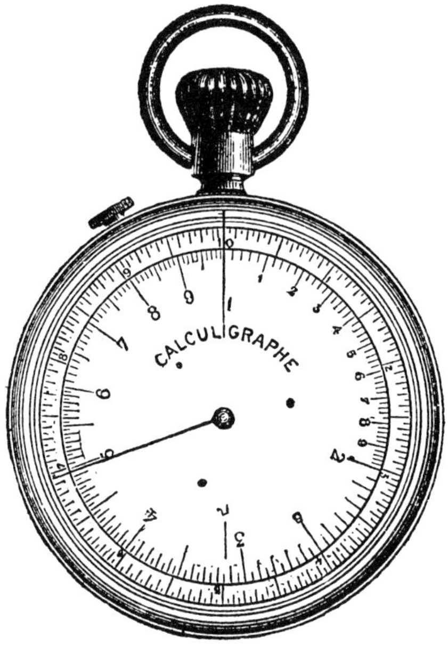

Figure 53

53), which has the appearance of a watch, the circular logarithmic scale can be moved by means of the "winder" under the fixed index, which remains at the 12 noon position. The needle forming the movable index is turned by the adjacent button. The second variant of the circular form, that of a fixed circle with two movable indexes, seems to have occurred in Oughtred's original apparatus, a modern version of which is due to Pierre Wiess.[7]

An admirable application of the helical scale is found in the *Spiral slide rule* of Professor George Fuller[8] of Belfast (1878) (*Figure 54*). In this device the first index is the end of a metal tongue *b* fixed rigidly to the handle *e* of the sleeve *f*. The movable index is the end *c* of a tongue *n* fixed rigidly to the cylinder *g*, which fits inside the sleeve *f* (and is held in any position there by friction) and which can be turned and slid so as to bring this index to any point on the helical scale. The scale itself is carried on a hollow cardboard cylinder surrounding the sleeve, which is also held in any given position by friction. The total length of the instrument, including the handle, is 42 centimeters (17 inches), while the length of the helical scale is 25.4 meters (83 feet 4 inches), giving the instrument an accuracy of one part in 10,000.

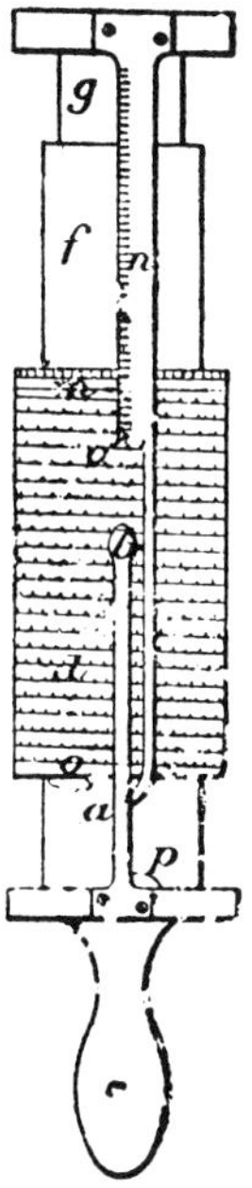

Figure 54

5.1.2: Adjacent Scales, Calculating Rulers

Suppose we have two rulers placed edge to edge and graduated along these edges with the same logarithmic scale. If the point 1 on one scale is opposite the point A on the other, the point B on the first will be opposite the point $A \cdot B$ on the second (*Figure 55*). This is because the distance on the second scale of this point from 1 is the sum of the distances from 1 to A on the first scale and from 1 to B on the second. As these two distances are proportional to $\log A$ and $\log B$, respectively, the full distance is proportional to $\log A + \log B$, which is equal to $\log(A \cdot B)$.

Notice that the numbers whose marks are opposite each other on the two scales are a kind of representation of the proportion

$$A/1 = C/B.$$

Thus if 1 on one ruler coincides with A on the other, all numbers B and C that coincide are in the above proportion. This is easily seen in *Figure 55* as

$$2/1 = 4/2 = 6/3 = 8/4 = 10/5.$$

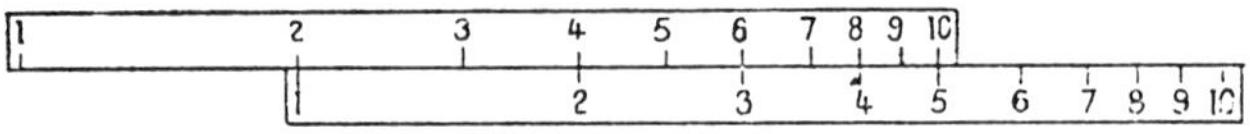

Figure 55

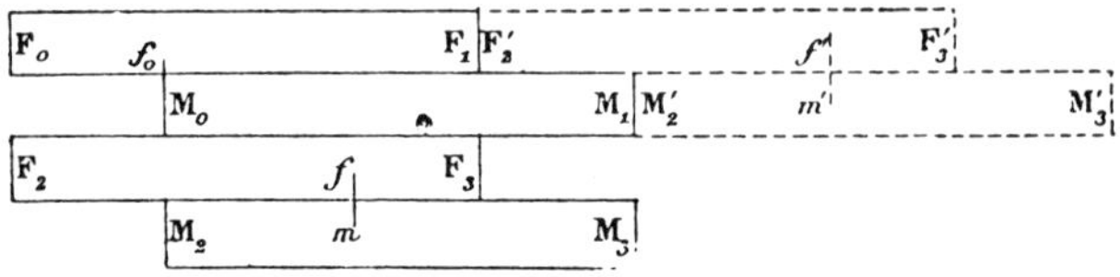

Figure 56

It was for this reason that the first devices of this type were called *proportional rules*: essentially they expressed proportions. When one of the terms in the proportion is set to 1 the corresponding second factor in the cross product is equal to the product of the other two.

It would seen that in order to give the product of any two numbers the upper scale would have to be extended: thus in *Figure 55* the products by 2 of all numbers greater than 5 fall beyond the upper ruler. However, the fundamental property of logarithms states that

$$\log(10 \cdot A) - \log A = \log 10,$$

from which it follows that the scale from 10 to 100 is identical to that from 1 to 10. Similarly the scales from 100 to 1000, from 1000 to 10,000, and so on, are identical to the scale from 1 to 10. It is therefore sufficient simply to repeat the scale from 1 to 10 on the upper ruler for the results to be obtainable in all cases.

Such an arrangement is usually attributed to Wingate,' but according to Professor Cajori[10] the credit should be given to Oughtred. It gives a significant improvement in accuracy over the use of either compass or dividers and was made still more useful by Seth Partridge[11] in 1671, who conceived the idea of a sliding rule of the same type as those that we use today.

Before going any further we should note that it is always possible, at the cost of a slight modification, to find the product of any pair of numbers set on the two rulers without needing to double the length of one of them. All that needs to be done is to *reverse* one of the scales, as illustrated in *Figure 56*. With this arrangement the relation between the three numbers is no longer the proportion given above, but rather

$$A \cdot B = C \cdot 1,$$

so that if A and B are set to coincide, their product is the number on one ruler opposite 1 on the other. If the 1 is outside the part common to the two rulers, the product, apart from a factor of 10, is given by the number opposite 10.[12]

Seth Partridge, the inventor of the slide rule as we know it today, had many imitators: Sauveur[13] in France (around 1700), Leadbetter[14] in England, and Lambert[15] in Germany (1761). But it was in England more than anywhere else that the use of this invaluable aid to the calculator spread most quickly,[16] where successive versions were made by Mountain (1778), Mackay (1802), and the brothers Jones (1814). It was a Jones instrument that the engineer and geographer Jomard introduced into France in 1815. Gunter's scales, and even rulers with juxtaposed scales such as those of Sauveur already mentioned and of Camus, which we shall describe later, had been used in our country well before this time, but the use of such instruments had not spread at all widely, and Jomard's importation was greeted as a novelty.[17]

Under the influence of Jomard, and also of Hachette, slide rules began to be manufactured in Lenoir's workshops around 1820. From this beginning the industry was bequeathed to Lenoir's successors, first Gravet-Lenoir and later Tavernier-Gravet.[18] These manufacturers have introduced successive improvements that have resulted in slide rules of unsurpassed precision. It is these workshops that have produced the majority of the slide rules used in France over the past three-quarters of a century. These slide rules have been of several types,[19] the most important of which have been the Mannheim slide rule (itself of two different types, one with folded scales and a cursor) (1851); the Peraux slide rule with fractional scales and two interchangeable slides (1860);[20] the slide rule, equipped with a lens, which was designed in response to the suggestions of Chief Engineer Lallemand for the Commission du Cadastre (1892); and finally the slide rule due to Beghin[21] (*Figure 57*), in which an ingenious arrangement enables the product of any three numbers whatever, or the quotient of any number by the product of any pair, to be found with a single setting of the device.[22]

Slide rules can have supplementary scales for use in particular applications.[23] The majority of instruments now in general use have trigonometric scales (logarithms of sines and tangents, usually on the back of the rule),

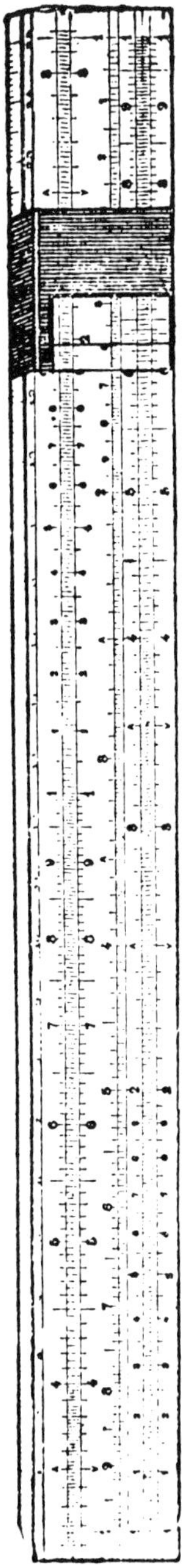

Figure 57

which are very useful, especially in the calculations required in surveying. Some have scales representing the logarithms of logarithms for calculating powers or roots of any order, among which are those of Roget[24] (1815), Burdon[25] (1864), Blanc,[26] and Schweth[27] (1901). Professor Furle has designed a slide rule[28] that has, in addition to the ordinary scale, a log-logarithmic scale and doubly and triply repeated scales with which equations of the 4th and 5th degree, trinomial equations of any order, and certain transcendental equations can be solved.

In order to perform various transcendental operations the slide rule has sometimes been provided with means for establishing given relations between the movements of the scales. It appears that Newton[29] was the first to have this idea when he conceived of a device for solving algebraic equations. Others who should be mentioned are F. W. Lanchester,[30] for a rule with a radial cursor, and Baines,[31] with a jointed parallelogram.

Calculating rulers have been made individually with special graduations to meet the needs of particular applications.[32] It is a striking fact that examples of such instruments were to be found in France at a time when the ordinary logarithmic device was not in general use. Examples of these special devices include Sauveur's gauging ruler, referred to above, Camus's (1741) for determining the capacity of a cask[33] from two linear measurements, and Gattey's (1799).

A Dutch engineer, F. J. Vaes, has designed a slide rule with several slides on which the scales are based on binary notation. He has been able to use these to calculate expressions involving several variables. Special mention must also be made of the very remarkable ruler he has designed for the calculation of the tractive force of locomotives.[34] A comparable instrument is the very ingenious ruler designed by Mr. Rieger for solving the problems arising in the design of reenforced concrete buildings.[35]

As a last example it should be pointed out that logarithmic scales are found combined with other devices in a variety of types of equipment. One example would be Lalanne's *arithmo-planimeter*,[36] which, although primarily intended for measuring plane areas, can, as the inventor himself has described, be used as a calculating instrument.

5.1.3: Calculating Grids, Cylinders, Circles, and Drums

The only way of improving on the accuracy of the slide rule is to increase the length of the logarithmic scales, but this usually results in an instrument of unreasonable size. In an attempt to increase the length of the scale while still keeping an instrument of convenient size, the fixed ruler and the slide can be divided into a number of equal length pieces and these arranged one below the other, the lengths of the fixed ruler alternating with those of the slide. The individual sections of the logarithmic scales can be rearranged either in one plane, giving what may be called a *calculating grid*, or along equally spaced lines along the surface of a cylinder, giving a *calculating cylinder*. Examples of the first form of this device are the *Universal Proportion Table* of Professor Everett[37] and the similar tables of Derivry (Calculation Card), Kloth[38] (on glass), Scherer,[39] and Proell.[40] Of the second type, a calculating cylinder, typical members are Mannheim's cylinder[41] (1851), which was the first of this type, Thatcher's *Cylindrical Slide Rule*,[42] and the *Rouleau calculateur* of J. Billeter.[43]

The circular arrangement of a logarithmic scale with an index, mentioned earlier, can be adapted to the form of two circular scales rotating, one over the other, about a common center. This has given rise to a large family of *circular calculators*, of which many were of French origin before the standard slide rule came into use. Examples would include the circles of Clairaut[44] (1727), Leblond[45] (1795), and Gattey[46] (1798). For contemporary examples from countries other then France we may examine Nystrom's *Calculator* (1854), the circles of Sonne,[47] equipped with a counter for the number of turns of the movable circle, Halden, F. M. Clouth,[48] John Fuller,[49] W. H. Hart,[50] which has a magnifying index, Steinhauser,[51] with spiral scales, F. A. Meyer,[52] with a counter like Sonne's, and Puller,[53] with a glass cursor and a magnifying lens. The French instruments that fall into this class include those of Renaud-Tachet,[54] Pouech,[55] Charpentier,[56] Beauvais, Arnault-Paisseau, and Appoulot, each having particular advantages that have been described in several publications. Most of these circular calculators, like the slide rules, have special scales[57] for operations involving squares, cubes, trigonometric functions, etc.

Not only can the two superimposed circular scales be written on rotating disks but they can also be put on the peripheries of a pair of contiguous drums mounted on the same axis. The first example of such a *drum calculator* is provided by Hoyau's box,[58] the cylindrical body and cover of which carry logarithmic scales on their peripheries. Other such devices have been proposed by R. Weber[59] (1872) and Beyerlen.[60]

The *ribbon calculator* of the Marquis de Viaris[61] can be included in this class of calculating instrument. It provides a very economical means of calculation when fairly rough approximations will suffice.

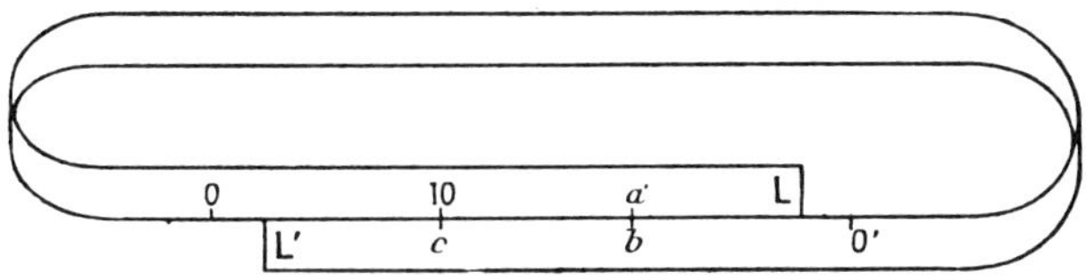

Figure 58

The ribbon arrangement (*Figure 58*) is the same as that of the reversed scale mentioned in connection with *Figure 56*. The two scales that are to be brought together are printed on a ribbon similar to a tailor's tape measure, the scales originating at each end of the tape. On one of these scales, at the exact point where the 10 is marked, is a metal hook through which the other end of the ribbon can be passed in order to keep the scales in contact. The point of the hook indicates, on the other scale, the number c, that is, the product of the two numbers a and b whose graduations have been brought together on the two scales.

5.2: Algebraic Machines

5.2.1: General Principles

In the *algebraic* machines, created and so named by Mr. Torres Quevedo, the functional scales on which the data are read are linked together by some mechanism that plays the same role as does the graphical linking in a nomogram. The inventor has given a completely general theory of these machines in his great memoir,[62] a truly fundamental work giving a rigorous proof of the possibility of translating *any* analytic relation (or set of simultaneous relations) into a mechanical system by a rational and precisely defined process.

Apart from the veritable jewel of ingenuity displayed by Mr. Torres in the design of his machines, attention should be drawn to the very original idea that has enabled him to graduate the scales corresponding to the different variables in such a way that the values over which these can range are practically unlimited. This idea consists of representing the value of each variable by the rotation of a disk graduated logarithmically from 10 to 100. In order to represent a number, the disk turns through an angle proportional to the logarithm of the number engraved on its peripheral

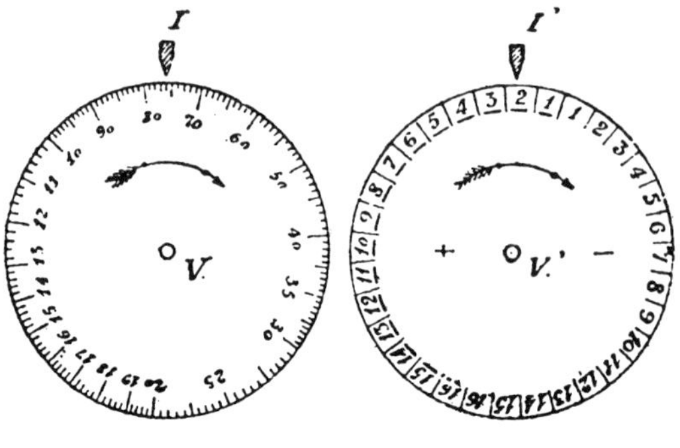

Figure 59

scale. Because the fractional part of the common logarithm is periodic over an interval lying between any two consecutive powers of 10, all that is needed to define the order of magnitude of the number corresponding to the reading on the disk is to add a second disk that counts the number of complete turns made by the first, thus acting as the characteristic of the logarithm. The two disks are shown separated in *Figure 59* when, in reality, they are actually coupled toegther. The graduations are read against the indexes I and I'. Torres has called this device the *logarithmic arithmophore*.

The graduation of the counter disk extends from -16 to $+16$, so that all numbers between 10^{-16} to 10^{+16} can be recorded. This can be regarded as a practically infinite range. In *Figure 59* the numbers opposite the indexes are 78.5^{63} and $+2$, respectively, meaning that the number recorded is 78.5. If the second index I' were pointing to -2, the number would be 0.785, while if to $+4$, it would be 7850, and so on.

It is quite simple to link two arithmophores to a third so as to perform multiplication; that is, the third will show the product of the numbers set on the first two. For this Mr. Torres has used a special type of gear train, which, since it has been used in automobiles, is known as a *differential*. Two identical bevel gears R_1 and R_2, whose axes are in the same line X, mesh simultaneously with a third bevel gear R whose axis A is in a sleeve that can turn about the line X of the common geometrical axis of R_1 and R_2. With this arrangement, if the gears R_1 and R_2 and the axis A turn through angles ω_1, ω_2, and ω, respectively, these are related by

$$\omega_1 + \omega_2 = 2\omega.$$

Thus, if R_1 and R_2 are connected to two identical arithmophores and A to a third for which the angular unit of graduation is half that of the first two (that is, graduated 10 to 1000 instead of the 10 to 100 graduations of the others), the numbers N_1, N_2, and N read from these respective dials will be related by

$$\log N = \log N_1 + \log N_2, \qquad \text{or} \qquad N = N_1 N_2.$$

Because of the logarithmic graduation, addition is less easily performed with arithmophores, but Mr. Torres has provided a remarkably ingenious solution to the problem, based on a mechanical interpretation of the principle of Gauss's addition logarithms. From the relation

$$\log(u + v) = \log v + \log[(u/v) + 1], \tag{1}$$

it can be seen that the problem is reduced to the same one discussed above if a way can be found of deriving $\log[(u/v) + 1]$ mechanically from $\log(u/v)$, because the latter is easily formed from $\log u$ and $\log v$ by means of the differential gears.

If we let $\log(u/v) = X$ and $\log[(u/v) + 1] = Y$, we have

$$Y = \log(10^X + 1). \tag{2}$$

The problem is therefore to link the two arithmophores so that their readings X and Y are related by equation (2). The graphical representation of this, taking X as abscissa and Y as ordinate, is a curve having the general form of a hyperbola whose asymptotes are the negative X axis and the bisector of the angle XOY. The curve approaches these asymptotes fairly quickly, so that beyond certain values $-\alpha$ and $+\alpha$ of the abscissa, which can be determined from the graph, it can be replaced by these lines to the degree of approximation required. It follows that it is only between the limits $-\alpha$ and $+\alpha$ for X that the ratio between the angular displacements X and Y needs to be allowed to vary. The passage from this observation to the practical solution of the problem involves a second observation of major importance. This also illustrates the type of difficulty with which the pure mathematician does not have to contend but which can present an insurmountable obstacle to the engineer seeking a mechanical solution to his problem.

The ratio of the angular speeds of the arithmophores X and Y is given by

$$dY/dX = 10^X/(10^X + 1).$$

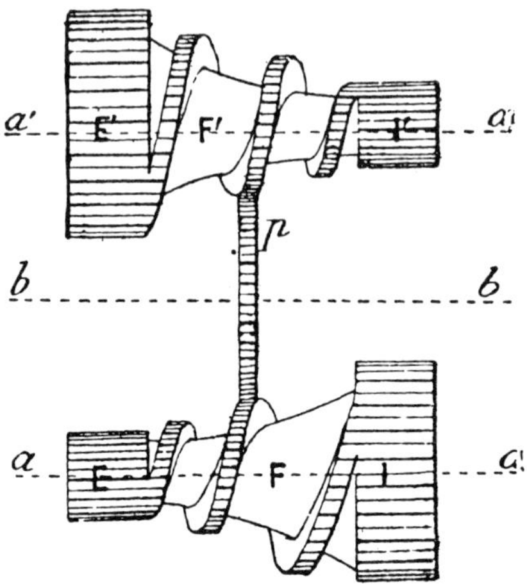

Figure 60

This tends to zero as X decreases indefinitely but, for practical purposes, can be taken to be zero after the value $X = -\alpha$. It is not possible to imagine a mechanism having this property, but the difficulty can be circumvented by writing the relation (2) in the form

$$Y = \log(10^X + 1) + mX - mX,$$

where the constant m is at our disposal, and to define

$$Y' = \log(10^X + 1) + mX, \tag{3}$$

$$X' = -mX. \tag{4}$$

The ratio of the angular speeds corresponding to (3) is

$$dY'/dX = 10^X/(10^X + 1) + m, \tag{5}$$

which remains finite and equal to m as X decreases indefinitely and, in practice, must remain at this value after $X = -\alpha$.

Mr. Torres has devised a mechanism to satisfy these conditions, which he calls *endless fusées*.[64] These are shown as F and F' in *Figure 60*. The profiles, determined by equation (3), have teeth cut on the helixlike curves that terminate in ordinary toothed wheels E and I on one member and E' and I' on the other. The connection between the two parts is made by the gear p in such a way that the ratio of the speeds varies from m, when p engages with E

and E', to $m + 1$, when it engages with I and I'. Between these two positions it varies according to equation (5).

The transformation from X to X' expressed by (4) presents no difficulty. Y can then be obtained from X' and Y' by means of a differential gear system because the relation is simply

$$Y = X' + Y'.$$

To conclude this chapter, we shall now show how Mr. Torres has combined his mechanisms so as to provide a completely general solution to the problem of finding, by mechanical means, the roots of any algebraic equations whatever.

5.2.2: Machines for Solving Equations

By a suitable grouping of terms, any algebraic equation with real coefficients can be put in the form

$$A_1 x^{m_1} + A_2 x^{m_2} + \cdots = B_1 x^{n_1} + B_2 x^{n_2} + \cdots, \tag{1}$$

in which each side consists of only positive terms.

If we now make the general substitution

$$x^{m_i} = X_i, \qquad x^{n_i} = Y_i \tag{2}$$

and make a logarithmic arithmophore correspond to each of the variables x, X_1, X_2, ..., Y_1, Y_2, ..., we can link each X_i or Y_i arithmophore separately to that for x so as to represent the relations (2), because this requires nothing more than to set the respective speed ratios to the constant values m_i, n_i.

Given this, we can use other arithmophores to form the products $A_i X_i$, $B_i Y_i$, using the method described above, and then use the endless fusées to form the sums $A_1 X_1 + A_2 X_2 + \cdots$ $B_1 Y_1 + B_2 Y_2 \cdots$ on two further arithmophores, which we will call A and B. As the arithmophore for x is turned, the values of $\Sigma A_i X_i$ and $\Sigma B_i Y_i$ can be read on A and B, respectively, and when these are equal the corresponding value of x is the root of the original equation.

This is the principle of Torres's machine for finding the real roots of algebraic equations with real coefficients.[65] The first model of such a machine, constructed by Torres himself, dealt with equations of either of the two forms

$$x^9 + Ax^8 = B \qquad \text{and} \qquad x^9 + Ax^7 = B.$$

Figure 61

This was only a simple demonstration model for showing at the Paris Académie des Sciences on 29, July 1895 (*Figure 61*). Mr. Torres has modified and improved the details considerably (*Figure 62*) since then.

Torres has also given a similar method for the mechanical solution of equations with imaginary coefficients, of the form

$$\sum A_m x^m = 0, \tag{3}$$

where

$$A_m = a_m(\cos \alpha_m + i \sin \alpha_m),$$

$$x = \rho(\cos \omega + i \sin \omega),$$

from which, by de Moivre's Theorem, we have

$$\begin{aligned} &\sum a_m \rho^m \sin(\alpha_m + m\omega) = 0, \\ &\sum a_m \rho^m \cos(\alpha_m + m\omega) = 0. \end{aligned} \tag{4}$$

The moduli ρ and a can be represented by logarithmic arithmophores and

Figure 62

the arguments ω and α_m by disks having ordinary angular graduations; the latter are termed *angular arithmophores.*

The method used is first to form, by means of the angular arithmophores, the sums $\alpha_m + m\omega = \theta_m$, which presents no difficulty. The formation of $\log a_m\rho^m \sin\theta_m$ and $\log a_m\rho^m \cos\theta_m$ encounters the difficulty that $\sin\theta_m$ and $\cos\theta_m$ can take negative values, but this can be circumvented by making a substitution similar to that described above, in which these functions are replaced by

$$c + \sin\theta_m - c \qquad \text{and} \qquad c + \cos\theta_m - c,$$

where c is any constant greater than 1. The two equations labeled (4) can then take the form

$$\begin{aligned} &\sum a_m\rho^m(c + \sin\theta_m) = c\sum a_m\rho^m, \\ &\sum a_m\rho^m(c + \cos\theta_m) = c\sum a_m\rho^m. \end{aligned} \tag{4'}$$

Torres has shown how, by means of an ingenious combination of a cam and an ecentric, the functions

$$\log a_m\rho^m(c + \sin\theta_m) \qquad \text{and} \qquad \log a_m\rho^m(c + \cos\theta_m)$$

can be constructed. The use of endless fusées then enables the logarithms of the sums on the left side of the equations (4′) to be found, a separate arithmophore corresponding to each of these sums; and the common right side is easily formed on a third arithmophore. If these three arithmophores are then linked so that their angular displacements are always equal, the arithmophores for ρ and ω will give the modulus and argument, respectively, of a root of the equation whose coefficients have, for modulus and argument, the values shown by the corresponding arithmophores.

The case of real coefficients reduces to the above example by taking arguments equal to 0 for positive coefficients or to π for negative ones.

The construction of the machine can be greatly simplified if it is designed to deal only with second-degree equations. The model constructed by Mr. Torres to deal with just this case has the added interest of illustrating how the values of a multivalued function are distributed around the critical points. This is a particular application of a very interesting idea of Torres, developed by him in a note to the Société Mathématique de France,[66] that of illustrating by means of movement certain facts from the field of analysis for which geometrical representation would not suffice.

Finding the imaginary roots of an algebraic equation with imaginary coefficients involves, as we have seen, the solution of a set of equations in two unknows, ρ and ω. It is clear that the type of method just described can be extended to give a means of mechanically solving sets of equations in any number of unknowns. It is also clear that the fusées, of the type devised by Torres for the mechanical representation of addition logarithms, can be made with other profiles in order to represent any other function. This means that the same method can be used to solve not only algebraic but also transcendental equations, in particular Kepler's equation. These points have been mentioned in order to give a glimpse of the rich possibilities flowing from the principles emanating from Torres's extraordinarily fertile imagination.

It should also be possible to attach a variety of other devices to these algebraic machines so as to enable them to solve certain equations with the aid of principles taken not only from mechanics but also from physics. Some examples of this type of device are those based on research in static equilibrium, such as that done by Berard[67] (1810), Lalanne[68] (1840), Exner[69] (1881), Boys[70] (1886), Massau[71] (1887), Grant[72] (1897); in hydrostatics, such as that developed by Veltmann[73] (1884), Demanet[74] (1898), Meslin[75] (1900); or even in work related to electricity, such as that of Félix

Lucas[76] (1888) and Arthur Wright. Others depend on the motion of roulette curves driven, by friction, by a uniformly rotating turntable—see, for example, Stamm[77] (1863), Marcel Deprez[78] (1871), and Guarducci[79] (1890)—or the action of articulated systems, such as that by Kempe[80] (1873).

For systems of linear equations, which are important in so many applications, very ingenious methods of solution have been given by Lord Kelvin[81] (Sir W. Thomson), Wehage,[82] and Guarducci.[83]

Notes

1. It would be logical to include in this class those very curious instruments for predicting astronomical events, probably first made by the Arabs and further developed and extended in Europe in the Middle Ages; a striking example is the *quadratum horarium generale* mentioned in Chapter IV during the discussion of the history of nomography. The devising of these instruments at a time when mathematics was so little developed shows remarkable ingenuity on the part of the inventors. [(Ed.) These instruments are usually classified under the name *astrolabe*.]

2. A summary of the history of logarithms is given in Appendix III.

3. The principle of *Gunter's line*, as it was then called, became known in France through Henrion's *Logocanon ou Règle Proportionelle* (Paris, 1626). Gunter's works were collected together and published by W. Leybourn [(Ed.) d'Ocagne spelled the name Leybourne] under the title *The Works of Ed. Gunter* (London, 1673). Schefelt made a set of Gunter's rulers at Ulm in 1699. A small book by Boissey de Bocage, printed in le Havre in 1683, explains the use of the logarithmic line put into the shape of a circle.

4. *Circle of Proportion* (London, 1632; Oxford, 1660).

5. *History of Logarithms*, by Hutton (prefacing his *Mathematical Tables*, 1811, p. 36). A helical scale was presented to the Académie des Sciences by Mr. Bouché (*C.R.*, 2nd Part, 1857). Mr. Malassis believes that Milburn's scale was a spiral rather than a helix.

6. *La Nature*, 1878, p. 31. Figure 53 represents a model with a modern simple scale. There are other models available with multiple scales.

7. *C.R.*, 2nd Part, 1900, p. 1289.

8. *Spiral Slide Rule, Equivalent to a Straight Slide Rule 83 Feet 4 Inches Long, or a Circular Rule 13 Feet 3 Inches in Diameter* (London, 1878).

9. *Construction, Description et Usage de la Règle de Proportion* (Paris, 1624); *Arithmétique Logarithmique* (Paris, 1626).

10. *History of the Logarithmic Slide Rule* (New York, 1909).

11. *The Description and Use of an Instrument Called the Double Scale of Proportion* (London, 1671). It was Haynes who constructed Partridge's instrument.

12. Beghin's rules, referred to later, have such a reversed scale. Mr. Malassis owns a ruler made by Collardeaux-Decheaume, dated 1820, with the same feature; this has two smaller rulers, one on the front and one on the back, and a special scale for cubes.

13. According to Lalanne (*Instruction sur les Règles à Calcul*, 1851, p. vii of the preface) he had rulers with slides made by the workers Gevin and le Bas. N. Bion's *Construction et Usage des*

Instruments Mathématiques (1752) contains a description of a logarithmic gauging ruler with a slide, due to Sauveur. In the Conservatoire des Arts et Métiers are two of Sauveur's logarithmic rulers made of copper, one of which is 1.40 meters long.

14. Wrongly given by some writers as the first inventor of the slide rule (**25**, p. 72).

15. *Beschreibung und Gebrauch des Logarithmischen Rechenstab* (Augsburg, 1761, 1772). Lambert's ruler, four feet in length, gave results correct to 1 part in 2,000; but Francoeur is wrong in regarding Lambert as the first inventor of the opposed-scales ruler (*B.S.E.*, 1821, p. 78).

16. Because they were originally made in Soho, these calculating rulers were for a long time called *Soho scales* or Soho rules in England. They are now spoken of as *sliding rules* or *slide rules*.

17. The calculating ruler was introduced into Austria around 1840 by Professors Adam Burg and Schultz of Strassnicki, and a few years later into Italy thanks to the work of Professor Quinto Sella, who published a very detailed study of the instrument, which was subsequently translated into French by Mr. Montéfiore Lévi (Liège, 1869).

18. It is a remarkable fact that Laplace, in his *Exposition du Système du Monde*, had foreseen the use of these logarithmic instruments before this attempt was made to introduce them into France.

19. A ruler designed by Lalanne and sold by Hachette in 1851, made of card and encased in glass, was intended mainly for the student's practice.

20. According to information provided by the Tavernier-Gravet Company, Péraux spent about 20 years developing his slide rule before making it available to the public. Another 2-slide ruler has been offered recently by Mr. Herrgott, who, like Mr. Péraux, has provided an account of his invention.

21. In a booklet specially written for the purpose, and which has gone quickly through several editions since its first appearance in 1899, Mr. Beghin has given a detailed description of his rule and has explained many of its uses. Not only has he given a very complete development of the theory but has also given a long series of applications to a variety of problems, in arithmetic, algebra, geometry, trigonometry, applied mechanics, physics, industrial chemistry, and even the textile industry. We may add here that, unknown to Mr. Beghin, a ruler of similar design was proposed in 1882 by Mr. Tcherepachinsky, a professor in Moscow; a single example was made by Tavernier-Gravet but the ruler remained unknown to the general public.

22. Mr. Favaro, continuing a list started by Sedlaczek in 1856, has catalogued the various types of calculating ruler (**25**, pp. 110–111). Apart from the special accounts issued by various inventors, in particular by Mr. Péraux and Mr. Beghin concerning their own designs, the calculating ruler has been the subject of many instruction manuals. Confining ourselves to those manuals written in French, and without any claim to completeness, we may list the following: Collardeau (1820); Ph. Mouzin (3rd edition, 1837); J. F. Arthur (1827, 2nd edition, 1845); Aug. Hadéry (1845); L. Lalanne (1851); F. Guy (3rd edition, 1855); P. M. N. Benoit (1853); a teacher of elementary mathematics (Fr. René) (1865); Montefiore Lévi (translated from the Italian of Quintino Sella, 1869); Labosne (1872); Claudel (1875); Gros de Perrodil (1885); Leclair (1902); Jully (1903); Dreyssé (1903); A. Vincent (1905); P. Rozé (1907); ourselves (1910, 2nd edition 1921); J. Bournisien (1917); J. Dap (1923); J. Lemoine (1925). J. F. Arthur further envisaged a special vernier for increasing the precision with which the scale could be read, but this has remained a theoretical curiosity (*B.S.E.*, 1851, p. 675).

23. Bour has shown that cubic equations expressed as trinomials can be solved easily with a rule having along one edge a logarithmic scale in which the intervals between divisions are double those of the scale on the other edge.

24. *Lond. Trans.*, 1815, p. 9 (*6*, p. 426, Note 756).

25. *C.R.*, Part 1, 1864, p. 573.

26. ***14***, p. 225; ***13***, p. 145.

27. *Zeitchr. Ver. Deutcher Ing.*, 1901, pp. 567, 720 (*6*, p. 427, Note 760).

28. *Zur Theorie der Rechenschieber* (*Wissenschaftliche Beilage zum Jahresbericht der Neumten Realschule zu Berlin*), 1899.

29. According to a letter from Oldenburg to Leibniz dated 24 June 1675, reproduced in *Opera Omnia de Newton* (Vol. IV, London, 1782, p. 520) and in Leibniz's *Mathematische Schriften* (First Part, Section I, Berlin, 1849). What is remarkable is that there is a striking similarity between Newton's method of solution and one of those given by Mr. Torres (*3*, Number 136).

30. *Engineering*, 7 August 1896, p. 172.

31. *Engineer*, 1 April 1904, p. 346.

32. Among rulers with special scales made by Tavernier-Gavet we may mention those due to the following: Moinot (1868), Goulier (1873), Sanguet (1888), and Bosramier (1892) for use in surveying; Montrichard (1876) for calculating the volume of timber in a wood; Lebrun (1886) for earthwork calculations; Gallice (1897) for nautical calculations, using the division of the circle into 240 degrees suggested by Mr. de Sarrauton; Leven (1903) for financial calculations; Mougnié (1904) for calculations of water flows using the formula due to Flamant. In 1895 the Forges et Aciéries de Saint-Chamond Company had a special rule made for calculating the speed, weight, and caliber of projectiles. New rules have been made more recently in response to certain industrial needs, in particular by Mr. P. Chessé for calculations concerning the central heating of houses.

Other rules for earthwork calculations have been made, for example, by Toulon (Durand-Claye, *Cours de Routes*, 2nd edition, p. 561) and Paulin (*Portefeuille des Conducteurs des Ponts et Chaussées*, Vol. XXI, 1889, p. 133).

For hydraulics calculations the W. F. Stanley Company of London made the Honeysett *Hydraulic calculating rule*, based on Bazin's formula; and Anthony's *Hydraulic calculator*, based on Manning's formula. Very recently (1927) the Pont-à-Mousson Company, manufacturers of blast furnaces and foundries, has produced a rule for hydraulics calculations based on Darcy's formula.

In July 1904 Mr. Wurth-Micha, an engineer in Liège, had a useful rule made for calculations concerning steam distribution. Finally we may mention the ingenious logarithmic ribbon calculator, due to Mr. J. Crevat (*Nature*, 1893, p. 378), by means of which the weight of a live farm animal can be found from three measurements.

33. Mr. P. Veyrac has recently designed a special rule for the same problem, ingeniously complemented by certain graphs for completing the calculation.

34. *3*, p. 135.

35. Published in Brno, Czechoslovakia, in 1924. A circular calculator, for the same application, designed by Mr. Deguillaume, was made by the Morin Company, which also made four different circular calculators to the design of Commandant Denis, for the machining of metals. All these circles are displayed in the Conservatoire des Arts et Métiers.

36. *A.P.C.*, Part 2, 1840, p. 3.

37. ***25***, p. 95.

38. *P.J.*, Vol. CCLX, 1886, p. 170.

39. *Logarithmisch-graphische Rechentafel*; Cassel, 1893, (***13***, p. 140; ***6***, p. 419).

40. *Zeitschr. Math. Phys.*, 1901, p. 218 (*6*, p. 420, Note 724).

41. The primative Mannheim cylinder is kept in the Conservatoire des Arts et Métiers. Although only 13.5 centimeters (5.25 inches) long it is equivalent to a straight slide rule of 2 meters (6 feet 8 inches).

42. ***13***, p. 141. For a description see *Zeitschr. für Vermessungswesen*, Vol. XX, 1891, p. 438 (***6***, p. 420, Note 727).

43. *Zeitschr. f. Vermess.*, Vol. XX, 1891, p. 346 (***6***, p. 421, Note 727).

44. *Hist. de l'Acad. des Sciences*, 1729, p. 142, and *Machines de l'Ac. des Sc.*, Vol. 5, p. 3.

45. *Cadrans Logarithmiques Appliqués aux Poids et Mesures*, Paris, 1799.

46. *Instruction sur l'Usage du Cadran Logarithmique*, Paris, 1799. The last two are identical, apart from a few details, with Glover's *Roue Arithmétique* (***25***, p. 73).

47. *Hannover Archit. Ingen. Ver Zeitschr.*, Vol. X, 1864, p. 452; ***13***, p. 142; ***6***, p. 423.

48. Made in Hambourg in 1872. ***13***, *Suppl.*, p. 3.

49. Called the *Computing telegraph*, first made in New York (***25***, p. 97).

50. Called a *Proportior*. See also *Techniker*, Vol. XXI, 1889–1890, p. 34 (***6***, p. 424, Note 741).

51. Made in 1893 in Munich. ***13***, *Suppl.*, p. 3.

52. Called a *Taschenschnellrechner*. *Mechaniker*, Vol. V. 1897. (***6***, p. 424, Note 742).

53. *Zeit. f. Verm. Weser*, Vol. XXX, 1901, p. 296 (***6***, p. 424, Note 743).

54. *G.C.*, 21 January 1893, p. 191.

55. This circle, dated earlier than 1890, was described in a special publication. It has scales marked on spirals, for calculating square and cube roots.

56. A first version of this circle had been sold under the name *Calculimetre*. The instrument is made entirely of metal and is of particularly careful construction.

57. By an ingenious linking of several logarithmic circles Mr. Malassis, whom we have mentioned several times already, has produced an instrument with which the weight per running meter and per square meter of a piece of cloth can be found immediately from measurements of its total weight, length, and width; this is a calculation that has to be done many times every day in weaving mills. The inventor has even attached his instrument to the balance on which the cloth is weighed, so that these numbers are given directly at the same time as the total weight.

58. *B.S.E.*, 1816, p. 150. It seems that the inventor had cylindrical snuff boxes made, of which the surfaces formed calculating drums.

59. *Anleitung zum Gebrauche des Rechenkreises*, Leipzig, 1875. ***13***, p. 142, and *Suppl.* p. 2.

60. ***13***, p. 143; ***14***, p. 230.

61. A former naval officer who graduated from the École Polytechnique in 1868 and died in 1901. He was known for his outstanding work in cryptography.

62. ***39***. An account of this fine work had been given by Mr. Appell (*C.R.*, 1st Part, 1900, p. 874). See also the Mémoires published by Mr. Torres in *A.F.A.S.* (1895 Congress), in *Revue de Mécanique* (Sept.–Oct. 1901) and in *Revue des Questions Scientifiques* (April 1902).

63. (Ed.) It appears more like 76 to the present editors.

64. (Ed.) The proper translation for "fusées" would be "a barrel of a capstan," but it seemed better to keep the French.

65. Clearly this gives only the positive roots; the absolute values of the negative roots are obtained by first changing x to $-x$.

66. *Bull. de la Soc. Math. de France*, Vol. XXIX, 1901, p. 167.

67. *Opuscules Mathématiques*, 1810.

68. *C.R.*, 2nd Part, 1840, p. 959.

69. ***6***, p. 434.

70. *Philos. Magaz.*, 5th Part, Vol. XXI, 1886, p. 241 (***6***, p. 435).

71. *Note sur les Intégraphes*, Gand, 1887, p. 30.

72. *Revue Technique*, 10 April 1897, p. 161. Grant's machine was perfected by Mr. Skutsch (***6***, p. 435).

73. *Zeitschr. Instrumentenkunde*, Vol. IV, 1884, p. 338. ***13***, p. 155.

74. *Mathesis*, 1898, p. 81. *Suppl. al Periodico de Mathematica*, May, 1898.

75. *C.R.*, 1st Part, 1900, p. 888. This very ingenious instrument consists of a number of suitably defined geometrical solids of rotation that can be suspended from points, whose positions are determined, on the beam of a balance and immersed in a liquid. The level of the liquid, when the beam is horizontal, gives the root of the equation.

76. *C.R.*, Part 1, 1888, pp. 195, 268, 587, 645, 1072.

77. *Essais sur l'Automatique Pure*, 1863, p. 43. This short book contains some very interesting observations on automatic generation, differentiation, and integration of functions.

78. *Notice sur les Travaux Scientifiques*, p. 5.

79. *Mémoires de l'Académie des Lincei*, Rome, 4th series, Vol. VII, 1892, p. 217.

80. *Messanger of Mathematics*, 2nd series, Vol. 2, 1873, p. 51.

81. *London Royal Society Proceedings*, Vol. XXXVIII, 1878, p. 111; also *Treatise on Natural Philosophy* by Thomson and Tate, 2nd edition, 1879, p. 482.

82. *Ver. Gewertfleiss Verh.*, Vol. LVII, 1878, p. 154 (***6***, p. 440, Note 307).

83. *Mém. de l'Acad. dei Lincei*, 4th series, Vol. VII, 1892, pp. 219, 225.

Chapter VI: Summary and Conclusions

Having reached the end of this survey, which has covered so large and so varied a number of mechanical and geometrical methods for aiding calculation, the reader may well be tempted to wonder whether such a richness and variety is really justified by the demands of practical needs, and whether it does not represent rather a mere multiplication of solutions to what is apparently the same problem.

We say "apparently" here with intent; in fact the different special conditions that apply in practical circumstances have the effect of making apparently identical problems very different indeed. In a financial organization, such as a bank or an insurance company, the greatest need is for simple operations such as multiplication or division performed on numbers having many figures, and here the use of arithmetical machines is strongly indicated. On the other hand, an architect carrying out a survey or an engineer designing some device may only need approximate results when manipulating numbers of a few digits length. In such a situation the logarithmic instruments, which would not have been suitable in the previous circumstances, have many advantages because of their relatively low cost and greater ease of use.

Again, if an engineer, accustomed as he is to using his ruler and set-square, needs to examine different arrangements of a structure whose strength and stability he is investigating, it is entirely natural for him to seek a method that will require no more effort than to make certain measurements on the drawings with which he is already working. In such a case a graphical method will be preferred to any other. If during some technical investigation a particular expression, perhaps complicated and requiring many arithmetical operations, has to be evaluated many times for values of its variables lying between certain limits, a natural course is to calculate a table of values for the expression, and this can then be put into the form of a table or a nomogram as is appropriate.

In a case such as the last, the tabular form should be used if there are not more than two variables and if the result is required to an accuracy of at least four figures. The nomogram form is to be preferred in all other cases because of the many reasons that have already been given in the section on nomography and that need not be repeated here. It is this form that simplifies approximate calculation in the widest variety of cases, however complicated the form of the calculation. It is our view that all technical workers are turning more and more to the use of nomograms for their calculations; the method allows the greatest personal choice, each user being free to select the method that he considers best suited to relieving him of labor.

It is no embarrassment to a good worker to be offered a rich variety of tools from which to choose the one best suited to the task he has in hand.

END OF THE MAIN TEXT

Appendix I: Tchebichef's Continuous Movement Arithmetical Machine[1]

AI.1: Description of the Machine

AI.1.1: The Adder

There are ten figure wheels, each with the sequence of digits 0 to 9 repeated three times around the periphery (*Figure 63*). These are mounted on a single horizontal axle and rotate under a cylindrical cover (*Figure 64*) in which there is a horizontal line of windows L in which, as we shall see later, the digits of the results can be read.

In each gap between a pair of wheels, and also at the right-hand end of the set, is a driving wheel R turned by means of teeth cut in its edge and moving the figure wheel located immediately to its left. The movement of the figure wheel has two components:

1. An angular rotation through a number of divisions equal to the value of the digit being added in the decimal place in question; this is proportional to the angular movement of the driving wheel.
2. A further angular movement determined by the carries originating from the additions in the lower-order positions and therefore from the figure wheels on the right of the one in question. This movement is such that when the wheel immediately on the right turns through ten divisions, the wheel in question turns through one division.

To obtain this composite movement, Tchebichef uses an epicyclic gear train[2] for each driving wheel, its gears engaging with toothed wheels that form an integral part of each of the pair of figure wheels between which this driving wheel is placed. The following conditions must be satisfied if the combination is to give exactly the total movement required:

1. The number of divisions (that is of gear teeth) of the driving wheels and the number of divisions of the figure wheels must be in the ratio 9 : 10; therefore the former have 27 teeth and the latter have 30.
2. The ratio of each epicyclic train must be 10; this is obtained by forming the train from one pair of wheels with 48 and 12 teeth engaging, respectively, with a second pair with 24 and 60 teeth, giving the ratio[3] $48/24$ times $60/12 = 10$.

The carries affect the positions of the figure wheels only gradually, as distinct from the effect in discrete movement machines; but as the angular deviation is always less than the distance between two consecutive figures,

Figure 63

Figure 64

the windows are made wide enough for the two figures to been seen at the same time and the true figure is thus always visible. Any possible ambiguity is removed by means of white bands marked on each figure wheel (see *Figure 63* and *Figure 64*), which take into account the angular deviations in the positions of the digits on the next wheel.

It is important that each driving wheel stop in a normal position, that is, with its teeth coinciding in position with certain horizontal lines on the cylindrical cover; this action is brought about by means of spring loaded stops.

For zeroizing, each figure wheel has on its right side a slot in which there is a notch, *E*, in the position corresponding to the start of each numbering (*Figure 63*). When a knob on the outside left-hand part of the machine is moved to the position marked *F* (*fermé*, closed), a row of hooks of lengths diminishing from right to left, all carried on the same bar, is positioned before the set of slots. The first hook on the right engages in the corresponding slot and when one of the notches comes into position engages with this and stops the wheel, which consequently shows the digit 0 in the window. The second hook, slightly shorter than the first, then engages with the slot in the second wheel and with a notch when one comes into position, and stops this wheel in the zero position; and so on. When all the wheels have been brought to zero positions the knob is moved to it other position, marked *L* (*libre*, free) and the hooks are disengaged from the slots so that the figure wheels are again free to turn.

For subtraction, all that is necessary is to reverse the direction of the rotation of the driving wheels.

AI.1.2: The Multiplier

Multiplication is done by repeated addition, the necessary repetitions being determined by the multiplier unit (*Figure 65*[4]), which is attached to the adder. The essential part of this unit is a set of steel rods, *A*, arranged longitudinally parallel to the axis of the adder's cylinder and each having a toothed wheel, *B*, at its left-hand end. The rods are of different lengths, so that each of these wheels engages with a different driving wheel of the adder; the wheels are of four teeth, specially shaped so as to mesh with the teeth of the driving wheels.

At the other end of each rod is a small gear (pinion), *P*, also having four teenth, free to slide along the rod but made to rotate with the rod by means of a projection that engages in a longitudinal slot in the latter. A cylinder,

Figure 65

C, whose axis is in line with that of the adder's cylinder, has nine sets of teeth projecting, respectively, from successive sections of its surface and able to engage with these pinions. Each of these sets of teeth has, in successive positions 9, 8, 7, . . . , 1 teeth, with no teeth being present in the position that would have been occupied by the tenth set.

Suppose one of the pinions is held in the position along its rod that corresponds to the position occupying 6 teeth on the cylinder. Each time one of its teeth is moved by a tooth on the cylinder, the wheel on the other end of the rod will move the corresponding driving wheel by 1 tooth, thus advancing the figure wheel by one position. When the cylinder has made one complete revolution the driving wheel will have advanced by 6 divisions. Sliding knobs on the cover of the machine (*I*, *Figure 66*[5]) enable the pinions to be set to positions corresponding to any given number, and thus any number can be set on the adder in a single turn of the cylinder *C*.

Because of the way in which the movements of consecutive pairs of figure wheels are related by the epicyclic trains, the two wheels of such a pair must not be moved simultaneously. To get over the difficulty represented by this constraint, the teeth on the central cylinder and those of the pinions are arranged in such a way that the former can never engage simultaneously with those of consecutive pinions. If we regard the successive pinions as being in odd and even positions, the arrangement is that as the cylinder turns the odd and even pinions are moved alternately. Finally, to remove all possibility of errors resulting from failure of the pinions, because of inertia, to stop at the required point, Tchebichef has shaped their teeth, and those of the cylinder, in such a way that the pinions are never free and therefore stop turning as soon as they are no longer engaging the teeth on the cylinder.

We can now see how the product can be formed of a multiplicand, set on the machine by means of the knobs, *I*, and a multiplier having several digits. With the adder placed below the multiplier, the handle is given a number of turns equal to the number of units in the highest-order decimal digit of the multiplier; the adder is then moved a distance equal to the spacing of a pair of driving wheels and the handle turned a number of times equal to the next lower-order digit, and so on.

It might seem that two handles would be required for this process, one to turn the central cylinder and a second to cause the adder to move to its new position. Tchebichef, however, has incorporated a mechanical linkage by means of which a single handle brings about the two movements, as follows. The handle drives an epicyclic train, and through this moves both the cylinder and a screw that advances the adder. These units must be moved alternately, and therefore the drives must be immobilized alternately. For this, there is on the front of the machine what is, in effect, a counter formed by toothed wheels, each having a finger, *d* (*Figure 66*), that can be moved to numbered positions in a slot. We shall call these wheels the *controllers*, because, as we shall show, it is they that control the movement.

A cursor *G* can be moved longitudinally, parallel to the axis of these wheels. When the finger on one of the control wheels is at the bottom of its slot, the position numbered 0, a notch in the wheel coincides in position with the finger of the cursor and is deep enough to allow the cursor to be moved past the wheel. When the same finger is in, say, position 5 in its slot the control wheel must turn through 5 divisions to bring the notch into line with the cursor.

The movement of the control wheels is linked to that of the central cylinder by means of a pinion carried by the cursor and engaging with a toothed drum that extends along the whole length occupied by the control wheels; this drum turns through the distance of one tooth when the cylinder

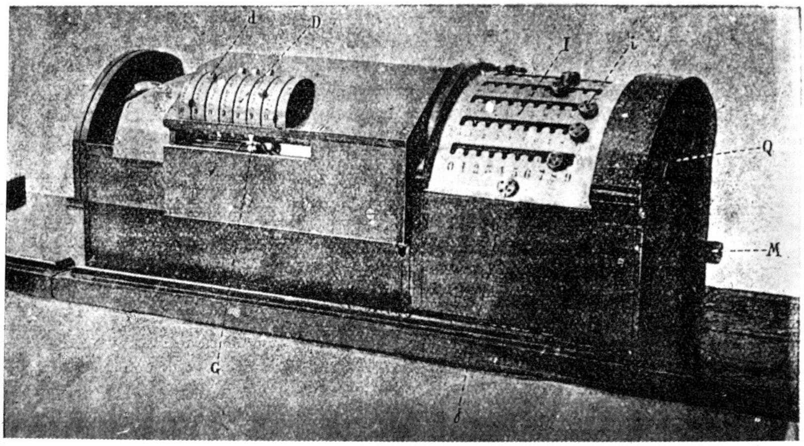

Figure 66

makes one complete turn. The movement of the cursor is linked to that of the screw that moves the adder. When the latter moves the distance between consecutive driving wheels the cursor moves the distance between consecutive control wheels.

As an example of how this combination of movements works, consider the multiplication of a number by 365. First, the fingers *i* of the first three control wheels on the left are set to positions 3, 6, 5, respectively, and the cursor *G* is moved as far as posssible to the left. The cursor is prevented from moving by the first control wheel, so the entire mechanical system linked to it cannot move and the screw cannot advance the adder; the movement of the handle is, therefore, transmitted to the central cylinder. At each turn of the cylinder the first control wheel, engaging the cursor's pinion, turns through one tooth, and after three turns its finger is at the bottom of the slot; this wheel is then prevented from turning any further and the movement of the central cylinder is stopped. But now the notch in the first control wheel is in line with the cursor finger and the cursor is free to move, and further turns of the handle cause the screw to turn and to move the adder. The process continues with the cursor being stopped by the second control wheel until 6 turns of the handle have been made in that position, and then by the third wheel until 5 turns have been made. Thus by continuous turning of the handle the multiplicand is multiplied first by 3, then by 6 in the next lower-decimal position and last by 5 in the position below that—in other words, by 365.

The method by which these various movements are brought about by a single handle is most remarkable from the theoretical point of view; but because of its complexity one cannot but wonder if it would not have been better, from the practical point of view, to have used two handles, as was implied, for the sake of simplicity, in the first part of the above explanation. One handle would drive the central cylinder, the other the screw mechanism for moving the adder's carriage; it could always be arranged that each was prevented from further rotation at the required instant, so that all one had to do was to change from one to the other as each in turn was found to have become immovable: that would be the only difference between this arrangement and what has been described above. The extra effort would be insignificant and, on the other hand, there would be the advantage of being able to turn the handle more quickly because of the simpler mechanism. This comment has Tchebichef's full approval, and it is for that reason that we have felt free to make it here.

AI.2: Instructions for the Use of the Machine[6]

AI.2.1: The Adder

AI.2.1.1: Zeroizing

It is assumed that the adder has been taken from the machine (which can be done by simply pulling it out) and placed in front of the operator so that the figure wheel digits that are currently showing through the windows can be read in their normal position. Setting the machine to zero is then performed as follows:

1. Move the knob, seen on the left of the machine, to the position marked *F* (*fermé*, closed).
2. From right to left in order, turn each driving wheel *R* (*Figure 64*) until it stops.
3. Free the mechanism again by moving the knob to the position marked *L* (*libre*, free).

If this last operation is not performed, it will be found that a stop prevents the adder from being reinserted into the multiplier.

AI.2.1.2: Addition

Adding a digit in the position corresponding to one of the figure wheels is done by selecting the projecting tooth of the associated driving wheel (on the right of the figure wheel) that is in the position, of the slot, bearing the required digit, and moving this tooth to the position marked zero. If one of the wheels is chosen to represent the units position, the tens, hundreds, etc., positions are then determined as the successive wheels on the left and a number of several digits is then added by operating in the same way with these successive wheels.

AI.2.1.3: Subtraction

For any one-digit position, this is done by selecting the tooth of the driving wheel that is in the 0 position and moving this to the position, in the slot, that is marked with the digit to be subtracted. The method is simply repeated, as described in addition, for a number of several digits.

To subtract one number from another, the adder is first set to zero, then the larger number is added, and finally the smaller number is subtracted.

AI.2.1.4: Reading the Result

Only one figure will appear in the first window on the right. Starting from there, the successive digits are given by the figures seen by following the white band from one figure wheel to the next on the left. Thus, in *Figure 64*, the number read is 3,191, 730,454.

AI.2.2: The Multiplier

AI.2.2.1: Zeroizing

It is assumed that the machine is in front of the operator, so that the digits set can be read in their normal positions. The handle, on the right, must be taken from its holding, an operation that can be done by applying a fingernail to its base. To set the machine up, that is, to attach the movable carriage to the fixed part when this has not been done already, the following operations are required:

1. Move the stud, seen on the right of the machine, to the position marked *R* (*retour*, return).
2. Turn the handle clockwise (as indicated by an arrow at *R*).
3. Return the stud to the position marked *A* (*aller*, go).

AI.2.2.2: Setting Up a Number on the Indicator

The *indicator* is the cylindrical cover *I* (*Figure 66*) at the right of the machine, with longitudinal slots in which there are notches numbered 0 to 9 from left to right. Knobs *i* can be moved along the slots and set in any of the notches; a slight rotation of a knob enables it to be removed from the notch in which it is placed, and so moved to any other in the same slot. The slots are numbered in the same way as the slots of the adder, that nearest to the front of the machine being number 1, the next to the rear number 2, and so on.

To set a number, the knob in slot 1 is moved to the notch numbered with the first digit of the required number, that in slot number 2 to the second digit, and so on. Thus the figures indicated in the successive slots show the number as it would be seen by an operator placed in front of the machine. Care having been taken to locate all the unused knobs in their zero locations, those that have been set are locked in their notches by a slight rotation in the direction opposite to that given in order to free them.

AI.2.2.3: Setting a Number on the Counter

The *counter* is the cylindrical cover *D* with circular slots, on the front of the machine. Below this counter is the cursor, *G*, which is free to move along a horizontal slide.

With the cursor at the right-hand end of its slide, a number is set on the counter in the normal decimal order by moving the knobs, *d*, to the appropriate numbered positions in their slots, the first slot on the left corresponding to the highest decimal order. The cursor must then be moved to the extreme left along its slide, as though to underline the number just set. In order to permit this leftward movement the knob must be pressed slightly forward.

AI.2.2.4: Multiplication

The adder and multiplier, having been set to zero by the operations noted above, are now joined together. The multiplicand and the multiplier are then set on the indicator and counter, respectively, as explained above, care being taken in the latter case to perform the "underlining" operation.

After having made sure that the stud has been set firmly into its position *A*, the handle of the machine is turned counterclockwise (indicated by an arrow at *A*) until *all the knobs of the indicator have returned to their initial positions and the screw driving the adder carriage starts to turn*. The result is then read in the windows of the adder unit.

AI.2.2.5: Division

First, the complement of the dividend is set on the adder, with the highest-order digit on the second figure wheel from the left. The multiplier unit is then set to zero and the two devices rejoined. The divisor is set on the indicator and all the knobs of the counter set to 9, taking care to "underline."

The handle is then turned as for multiplication (arrow *A*), but halted at each successive decimal order at the instant when the number seen on the adder is about to change from a 1 on the extreme left followed by 0s on all other positions; if this point is overshot, it can be restored by a single turn of the handle in the reverse direction. The cursor is then pushed forward so that it can move past the counter wheel with which it is in contact and, at the same time, the handle turned so as to move the adder carriage. After it has passed the wheel, the cursor is allowed to return to its normal position and continue moving until it reaches the next counter wheel.

When all the digits of the multiplicand have been dealt with in this way, the figures given by the positions of the counter knobs are the 9's complements of the quotient and the number seen in the windows is the complement of the remainder. The decimal point must be put after the figure whose decimal order, going from left to right on the counter, is one greater than the difference between the number of figures in the dividend and the number in the divisor.

These rather subtle points will be made clear by means of an example. Suppose I wish to divide 236,548 by 3141. I must first set the complement of the dividend on the adder, leaving the first position on the left blank; that is, I set 0,763,452,000 on the adder and I then attach the adder to the multiplier unit.

Next I set 3141 on the indicator, bring the counter knobs all to 9 and "underline" with the cursor.

I note that a single turn given to the cylinder while the cursor is in contact with the first wheel would take the result beyond the desired 1,000,000,000 because this would add 3141 to 7634; so I cause the cursor to move past this first wheel by turning the handle and so advancing the carriage. With the cursor in contact with the second wheel I continue turning until I see in the windows the number 0,983,322,000 because at this point one further turn would add 3141 to 8332, passing 1,000,000,000 again. I therefore cause the cursor to pass the second wheel and start again with the third, stopping when I see 0,999,027,000; and with the fourth until I see 0,999,969,000.

If I finish at this stage, the remainder is 307 and I read in the counter 9,246,999, so that the digits of the quotient are 0,753,000. Since the dividend has two more figures than the divisor I must put the decimal point after the third figure of the quotient, which is therefore 75.3.

AI.2.2.6: Restowing the Handle

This operation is done by pressing with the finger on stop Q (*Figure 66*), the head of which is seen on the disk driven by the handle.

Notes

1. During his last visit to Paris in May 1893 Tchebichef (we have transliterated his name in the way he has suggested) had his machine completely dismantled and reassembled in front of us by a member of the Gautier Company, by whom it was built. This was to enable us to write the account given here, which he has read carefully and has approved.

2. The wheels of these gear trains are partially visible in *Figure 63*.

3. (Ed.) This ratio was incorrectly given as 48/24 times 60/13 = 10 in the original edition.

4. *Figure 65* shows the multiplier unit partially dismounted, after removing the cylindrical cover with longitudinal slots and the counter with transverse slots (*Figure 66*).

5. (Ed.) This was noted as *Figure 65* in the original text.

6. (Ed.) The French of this whole section is written in a style completely different from that used in the other parts of the book. The difference is so striking that we speculate the section may have been written by Tchebichef himself, or perhaps d'Ocagne copied down the instructions as Tchebichef described the workings of the machine during the time the two of them examined the machine in 1893 (see endnote 1).

Appendix II: A Note on the Scheutz Difference Machine[1]

Let u be a function of x that for equidistant values

$$x, x + \Delta x, x + 2\,\Delta x, x + 3\,\Delta x, x + 4\,\Delta x, \ldots$$

takes values that we denote by

$$u_0, u_1, u_2, u_3, u_4, \ldots.$$

The difference, $u_{n+1} - u_n$ between any value and its predecessor u_n is written Δu_n, so we have the series of first differences

$$\Delta u_0, \Delta u_1, \Delta u_2, \Delta u_3, \ldots,$$

and similarly the second differences

$$\Delta^2 u_0, \Delta^2 u_1, \Delta^2 u_2, \ldots,$$

of third differences

$$\Delta^3 u_0, \Delta^3 u_1, \Delta^3 u_2, \ldots,$$

and of fourth differences

$$\Delta^4 u_0, \Delta^4 u_1, \ldots,$$

which is as far as we shall go here.

To go in the opposite direction, we have seen (in that part of Chapter I that dealt with Difference Machines) that if we know the values

$$u_0, \Delta u_0, \Delta^2 u_0, \Delta^3 u_0$$

and the series of fourth differences

$$\Delta^4 u_0, \Delta^4 u_1, \ldots,$$

we can derive the values of

$$u_1, \Delta u_1, \Delta^2 u_1, \Delta^3 u_1,$$

because we have, by addition,

$$\Delta^3 u_1 = \Delta^3 u_0 + \Delta^4 u_0, \qquad \Delta^2 u_1 = \Delta^2 u_0 + \Delta^3 u_0,$$

$$\Delta u_1 = \Delta u_0 + \Delta^2 u_0, \qquad u_1 = u_0 + \Delta u_0.$$

The values of the group

$u_2, \Delta u_2, \Delta^2 u_2, \Delta^3 u_2$

can then be calculated by a second series of additions, and so on.

This is the procedure that is normally followed in hand calculation and in essence is that used in constructing the *Tables de Cadastre* under the direction of Prony (see Appendix III, which describes the history of logarithms). It can, however, be modified slightly as follows.

If we start with the group of values

$$u_2, \Delta u_1, \Delta^2 u_1, \Delta^3 u_0 \qquad (1)$$

together with, as always, the series of fourth differences

$$\Delta^4 u_0, \Delta^4 u_1, \Delta^4 u_2, \ldots,$$

then a first series of additions gives

$$\Delta^3 u_1 = \Delta^3 u_0 + \Delta^4 u_0, \qquad \Delta u_2 = \Delta u_1 + \Delta^2 u_1,$$

and using these results a second series of additions gives

$$\Delta^2 u_2 = \Delta^2 u_1 + \Delta^3 u_1, \qquad u_3 = u_2 + \Delta u_2,$$

thus replacing the group (1) values by

$$u_3, \Delta u_2, \Delta^2 u_2, \Delta^3 u_1, \qquad (2)$$

in which all the subscripts have been increased by 1. This process can be repeated indefinitely to produce the values u_4, u_5, u_6, etc. It is this procedure that is used in the Scheutz machine.

We shall not attempt to explain the working of the Scheutz machine in any detail because it would require too many diagrams to explain the function of the large number of separate parts. What we shall attempt to do is to give a reasonably close account, using the well-known method of showing rotating objects by projecting their shapes on the plane. In these projections a gear wheel becomes a toothed rack and rotation becomes translation. The essential part of the Scheutz machine is represented in *Figure 67*, where racks C_0, C_1, C_2, C_3, C_4 correspond to toothed rings. If only differences up to the fourth order are used, the rack C_4 need not have teeth. The tongues T_{01}, T_{12}, T_{23}, T_{34} correspond to the figure wheels that can be seen in *Figure 25*; as these wheels are all keyed on the same vertical axis the tongues all move together, from left to right and then from right to left.

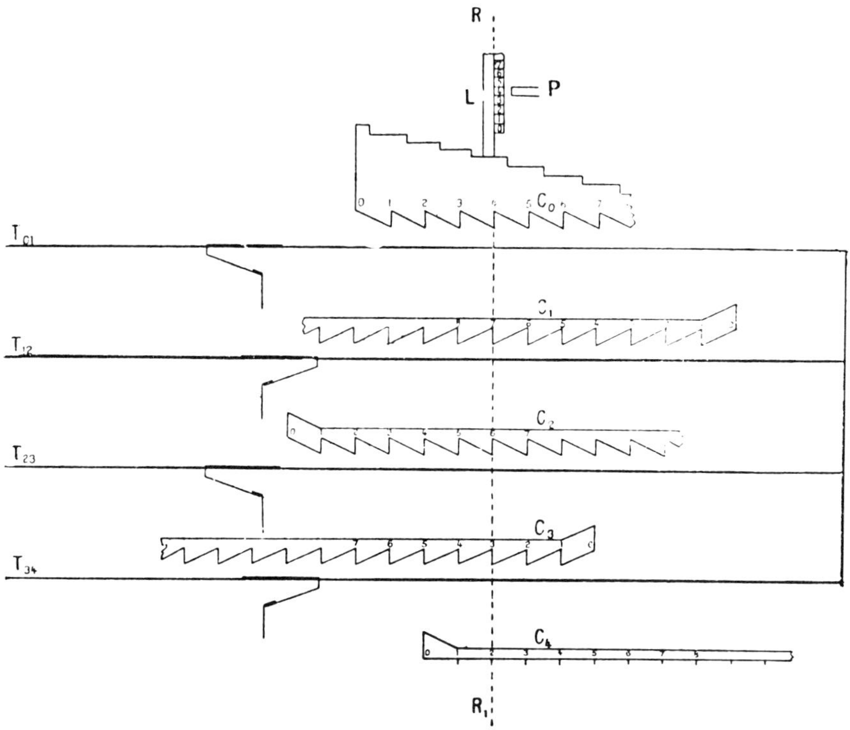

Figure 67

The mechanism for performing the successive additions of the differences, which we shall call the *adder*, appears in this transformation as the element *abcdef* in *Figure 68*. This addition mechanism pivots about the point *c* at a joint fixed to the tongue. The arm *ef* hangs freely and pivots about the point *e* in such a way that if a force is applied in the direction *gh* the arm alone moves, but if in the direction *hg* the whole element turns about *c*. In this latter event the arm *bk*, pivoted at *b*, is raised like a flag and remains in that position, even if the pressure on *ef* is removed, engaging with the rack above (*Figure 69*). As *bk* crosses the vertical line RR_1 of *Figure 67* (due to the tongues being moved back and forth) it strikes a finger, which turns it over and so allows the adder to return to the position shown in *Figure 68*.

Having explained the elementary movement of the adder mechanism, let us now return to *Figure 67*. Suppose the values of the even differences $\Delta^4 u_0$, $\Delta^2 u_1$ and the function u_2 are set by moving the racks C_4, C_2, C_0, respec-

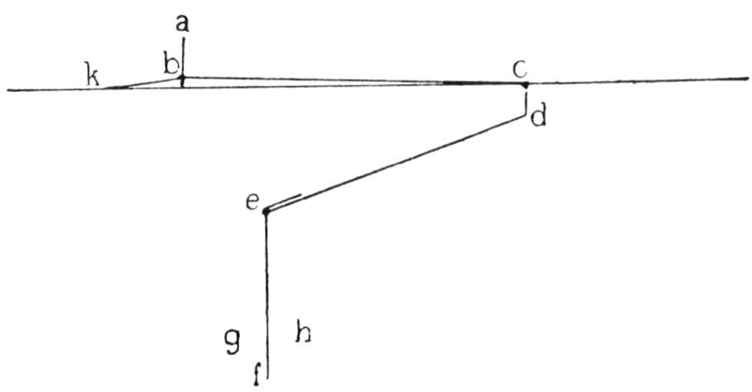

Figure 68

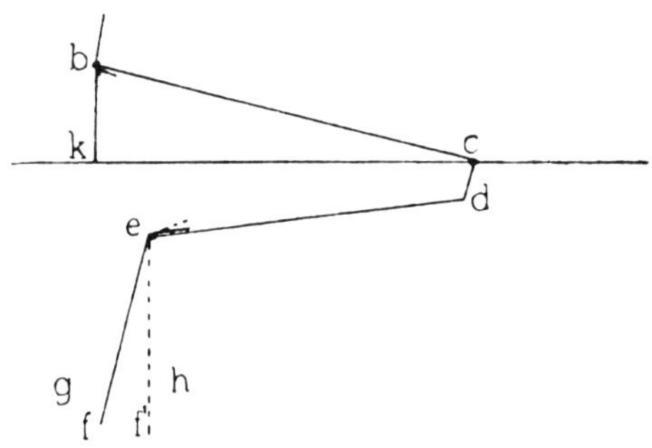

Figure 69

tively, the appropriate number of teeth to the left (taking the line RR_1 as the zero point); and the odd differences $\Delta^3 u_0$, Δu_1 by moving racks C_3, C_1, respectively, to the right; then we shall have the situation show in *Figure 67*, namely,

$$\Delta^4 u_0 = 2, \qquad \Delta^3 u_0 = 3, \qquad \Delta^2 u_1 = 6, \qquad \Delta u_1 = 7, \qquad u_2 = 4.$$

If the complete tongue assembly is now moved from left to right, the following operations will be performed. The adder attached to T_{34} will be raised when it encounters the stop at the end of the rack C_4 (at a position $\Delta^4 u_0$ steps to the left of RR_1); it will remain raised during part of the left-to-right motion and will therefore cause the rack C_3 to move $\Delta^4 u_0$ steps to the right (two steps in the situation shown in *Figure 67*). C_3 will then register the number

$$\Delta^3 u_0 + \Delta^4 u_0 = \Delta^3 u_1.$$

Similarly the adder on T_{12}, raised by C_2 over a move of $\Delta^2 u_1$ steps, moves C_1 by this number of steps, so that this rack now registers

$$\Delta u_1 + \Delta^2 u_1 = \Delta^3 u_1.$$

The left-to-right movement is now followed by one from right to left that, by exactly the same process, results in

$\Delta^2 u_1$ increased by $\Delta^3 u_1$, giving $\Delta^2 u_2$,
u_2 increased by Δu_2, giving u_3,

so that the original group of values (1) has been replaced by (2).

This account shows that the Scheutz machine belongs to the class of variable action machines defined in Chapter I.

The remaining action of the machine is to print the value u_3. To accomplish this, the rack C_0 carries a stepped metal wedge (see *Figure 67*) of which the heights of the successive steps are proportional to the numbers $0, 1, 2, \ldots, 9$, on which rests the lower end of a tongue having these numbers embossed on a vertical line on one side; the distance between consecutive numbers is the same as the height of each step. A lead slug, P, is held in an appropriate fixed position, and when pressed receives the impression of the figure then opposite this position.

If this entire mechanism is replicated 15 times, with the addition of a carry mechanism, then numbers of up to 15 digits can be handled while needing only 10 teeth on each rack. The carry mechanism is essentially the same as that used in the other arithmetical machines described in this book. The printing tongues (in reality, wheels) are arranged side by side and their digits aligned so that the required numbers are imprinted on the lead slugs.

If the machine is used to calculate values of a polynomial of at most fourth degree, then the fourth difference is always a constant and there is no need to move rack C_4 (which is, of course, actually a ring). In this situation all the numbers are correct to the fifteenth figure. In general, however, the function to be evaluated is more complicated than a fourth-degree polynomial, and this means that the fourth difference will vary slowly. This, in turn, will have the consequence that errors will accumulate in the third, second, and first differences and, eventually, in the function value itself; this results in an increasing number of digits, reading from the right, being in error. This is dealt with by printing only the first seven digits, reading from the left, of each function value and operating the machine in this way only as long as the error does not affect the eighth digit. The number of function values that can be produced before the error affects the eighth digit can be calculated in advance. After this number has been produced, new starting values are found and the machine reset before the whole process is repeated.

Note

1. The form of this description is due to Engineer-Colonel Bertrand.

Appendix III: A Summary of the History of Logarithms

The fundamental and universal importance of logarithms as a means for simplifying calculation is such as to merit a short note on their history.[1]

The original observation that led to the idea of logarithms is the following: Let two number sequences be written in parallel, one a geometric progression starting with 1, the other an arithmetic progression starting with 0. If A, B, C are any three terms of the geometric series and a, b, c the corresponding terms of the arithmetic series, then if

$$A \times B = C,$$

it follows that

$$a + b = c.$$

This property was noticed by Archimedes in connection with a problem in which he needed to find the decimal order of magnitude of an immense number.[2] At the beginning of the 16th century it was attributed to Michael Stieffel (1486–1567). The two series were, initially, limited to progressions consisting entirely of integers. This had to be modified, in the case of the development of logarithms, by the idea of interpolation between the consecutive integer terms.

This happy idea sufficed to immortalize the name of the Scottish John Napier, Baron of Merchiston, who divided his time between theology and mathematics. Not content with having conceived the idea, he had the virtue of turning it to practical use by calculating the first table.[3] This table,[4] although containing several errors, was sufficient to demonstrate the capabilities of the new invention.

It is worth recalling that one of the first and most enthusiastic of those to take up this new method of calculation was the illustrious Kepler, who, without this aid, would very likely have abandoned the calculation of the tables from which he was able to infer the laws of motion of the planets. If logarithms had not been invented at that time, the law of universal gravitation might still be waiting to be discovered!

Napier's logarithms suffer from the practical disadvantage that they are taken to an incommensurable base. This means that if a number is multiplied by 10, its logarithm is not increased by 1 but rather by the incommensurable base of Napier's first logarithms. Napier himself was aware of the value of taking 10 as the base for logarithms, but died before he was able to make this change. He had done no more than tell his son of his plans, and it is to Henry Briggs, a professor at Oxford,[5] that the honor of being the first to calculate the new logarithms must be given. It is these that, under the name of *common logarithms*, are used everywhere today.

Briggs had the fortitude to calculate, to 14 decimal places, the values of the logarithms of the numbers from 1 to 20,000 and from 90,000 to 100,00.[6] It was left to the Englishman Gellibrand to produce the logarithms of the trigonometric functions[7] and the Dutchman Vlacq to fill the gap between 20,000 and 90,000. Briggs's tables, completed by Vlacq and published in 1628,[8] have been a veritable treasure store on which all later table makers[9] have drawn, needing to do no more than reduce the original number to 7, 6, 5, 4, or even fewer figures, according to the degree of approximation they needed.

Scarcely any progress has been made since Vlacq in the tabulation of logarithms except in points of detail concerning the layout of the tables, the grouping of numbers, the arrangements for giving greater ease of reading, and finally the precision to which the values are given.[10] The greater the number of digits in a logarithm, the greater the opportunity for error; however, the use of difference machines for calculating logarithms and the invention of stereotyping, which allows errors to be corrected as they are found without the risk of introducing new ones, has helped to eliminate these opportunities for errors.

It would take too much space to review the more than 500 tables that have been published in all the countries of the world. We shall, therefore, limit ourselves to summarizing what has been done in France.

Napier's own works (*Mirifici Logarithmorum Canonis Descriptio* and *Constructio*), which include tables of logarithms of trigonometric functions, were published in Lyons in 1620. Briggs's tables were imported into France in 1624 by Wingate, whose contribution to the development of the calculating rule has been questioned earlier in Chapter V. Gardiner's tables, given to 7 decimals, were published in Avignon in 1770 in an edition that was highly prestigious but, being of full folio size, not easy to handle. These were then completed and published by Callet in 1783, in a very portable volume that does credit to the skillful printer Ambroise Didot. It was at the time of a new edition, in 1795, that Ambroise's son Firmin invented the process of stereotyping, and the volume produced by this method, in a rather larger format than its predecessor, became famous and is still being reprinted. Another edition of these tables, less well known and in much smaller format, was published by Lalande in 1805, again printed by Didot. With these tables Lalande was able to show the advantage of using logarithms to five decimal places for ordinary calculations.

All these publications were essentially copies of Vlacq's work and, whatever their practical value may have been, their scientific status was eclipsed by the great enterprise undertaken in France at the end of the 18th century in response to the adoption of the metric system. The new division of the quadrant into 100 parts required new tables to be calculated, and Prony, to whom the responsibility for the compilation was given, organized the work in a most remarkable way.[11] He divided his team of workers into three groups: the first group consisted of a small number of famous geometers, including Legendre, who developed the formulae to be used; the second was a group of mathematically trained calculators who laid out these formulae for calculation and filled in the first horizontal line and the last vertical column on each page; the last consisted of about 60 simple artisans who could do no more than add, but with the method of differences this was sufficient for them to be able to complete the remaining columns on the page.[12] All the calculations were taken to 14 decimal places and were done twice, in different locations, as a check.

These tables were known as the *Tables du Cadastre*; their printing was undertaken by Didot, but had to be stopped when a general currency collapse ruined the French economy. The 8-decimal-place tables used by the Army and the *Service Géographique* were subsequently derived from these; they were printed by the *Imprimerie Nationale*, with characters specially engraved for the purpose, in a volume that is still unrivaled for beauty of production.

If calculations of very high precision have to be performed on very large numbers, the method developed by Fedor Thoman,[13] which involves factorization, enables the logarithm of any given number, and conversely the number corresponding to any given logarithm, to be obtained to 27 decimal places with about twenty lines of calculation. If, on the other hand, approximations of low order will suffice, graphical tables of logarithms can be used.[14] These graphical tables are essentially the same two scales (one giving the numbers and the other their logarithms) as were described earlier for Gunter's line of numbers. It is possible to cut these scales into sections and arrange these in the form of a table. This arrangement has the advantage of removing all need for calculation of interpolated values, interpolation here being done entirely by eye.

Mr. Pouech has also made such a graphical table of logarithms, but this time with the scales on concentric circles.

Notes

1. We owe to Engineer-Colonel Bertrand the references that have enabled us to write this note.

2. *Traité de l'Arénaire* (complete works of Archimedes, translated into French by Peyrard, p. 360).

3. *Mirifice Logarithmorum Canonis Descriptio* (Edinburgh, 1614). This quarto volume of 56 pages of text and 90 pages of tables is dedicated to the Prince of Wales, later the unfortunate Charles I. It ends with the sentence "Interim hoc brevi opusculo fruamini, Deoque opifici summon omniumque bonorum opitulatori laudem summam et gloriam tributite" ("In gathering the fruits of this little work, pay tribute to the glory and bounty of God, sovereign author and giver of all blessings").

4. (Ed.) Actually a table of the logarithms of sines, rather than the logarithms of natural numbers.

5. (Ed.) Actually a professor at Gresham College in London at the time he was working with Napier, although he very soon became a professor at Oxford.

6. *Arithmetica Logarithmica* (London, 1624).

7. *Trigonometria Britannica* (Gouda, 1628).

8. *Arithmerica Logarithmica*, 2nd edition (Gouda, 1628).

9. Including the Chinese, for certain of their tables, which they claim are of great antiquity, contain the same errors as those of Vlacq, which leaves no doubt as to their true origin. Vega's *Thesaurus* (1794) is also a copy of Vlaq.

10. One can only regard as scientific curiosities the *tours de force* of certain dedicated individuals who have driven themselves to calculate logarithms to an extraordinary number of decimals: Wolfram to 48, Sharp to 61 decimals!

11. See the note by Prony about the tables in *Mémoires de l'Institut* (Sciences Math. et Phys.), Vol. V, Fructidor year 12 (1804), p. 49. [(Ed.) Fructidor year 12 means the 12th month of the 12th year of the French Republic.]

12. It is said that the majority of the members of this third group were wig makers who had been thrown out of work as a result of a change in fashion.

13. *Tables de Logarithmes à 27 Décimales pour les Calculs de Précision* (Paris, Imprimerie Impériale, 1867). Gardiner had already provided tables to 20 decimals for high-precision calculations. Similar tables to 12 decimals, based on a different principle, had been published in Brussels in 1877 by Mr. Namur, with an interesting introduction on the theory by Mr. Mansion.

14. *Tableau Métrique de Logarithmes*, by C. Dumesnil (Paries, Hachette, 1894). The same author has produced, in 1900, a *universal ruler* in the form of a spiral, which may be compared with the "graphical calculator" of H. Gudoux.

Bibliography[1]

Main Works of the Author That Concern the Subject of the Present Volume

1. *Prodédé Nouveau de Calcul Graphique* (*A.P.C.*, November 1884, p. 73).

2. *Nomographie. Les Calculs Usuels Effectués au Moyen des Abaques. Essai d'une théorie Général* (G.-V., 1891).

3. *Traité de Nomographie* (G.-V., 1899; 2nd edition 1921).

4. *Exposé Synthétique des Principes Fondamentaux de la Nomographie* (*J.E.P.*, 2nd series, Vol. VIII, 1903, p. 97).

5. *Calcul Graphique et Nomographie* (Doin, 1907; 3rd edition 1924).

6. *Calculs Numériques* (Vol. I, Book 4, Section 3 of *Encycl. des Sc. Math.*; adapted from an article of R. Mehmke in the German edition of the same encyclopedia; Tubner and G.-V., 1909).

7. *Cours de Géométrie Pure et Appliquée de l'École Polytechnique* (2 Vol.; G.-V., 1917–1918).

8. *Principes Usuels de Nomographie, avec Application à Divers Problèmes Concernant l'Aviation et l'Artillerie* (G.-V., 1920).

9. *Vue d'Ensemble sur les Machine à Calculer* (G.-V., 1922).

10. *Esquisse d'Ensemple de la Nomographie* (Section IV of *Mémorial des Sc. Math.*; G.-V., 1925).

Works of Other Authors Cited in the Text

Mechanical Calculation

We should recall that it was the first edition of the present work that first gave a rational classification of calculating machines.

11. C. Dietschold. *Die Rechenmaschine* (Leipzig, 1886).

12. Ch. Babbage. *Calculating Engines* (London, Spon,[2] 1889). A collection of manuscript notes left by Babbage and published by his son. The work is available in the Conservatoire des Arts et Métiers.[3]

13. W. von Dyck. *Katalog Mathematischer und Mathematisch-physikalisher Modelle Apparate und Instrumente* (Munich, 1892 and 1893).

14. W. von Bohl. *Instruments and Machines for Mecahnical Calculation* (in Russian), Moscow, 1906.

15. L. Jacob. *Le Calcul Mécanique* (Doin, 1911).

16. L. R. Dicksee. *Office Machinery* (London, Gee and Co., 1917).

17. J. A. V. Turck. *Origin of Modern Calculating Machines* (Chicago, West. Soc. of Eng., 1921).

18. Martin. *Die Rechenmaschinen und ihre Entwicklungs Geschichte* (Pappenheim, J. Meyer, 1925).

Graphical Calculation

19. B. E. Cousinery. *Le Calcul par le Trait* (Paris, Carillan-Gaury et Dalmont, 1839).

20. K. Culmann. *Die Graphische Statik* (Zurich, Mayer and Zeller, 1866). The first translation

of this book was by Glasser, Jacquier, and Vala (Paris, Dunod, 1880) from the 2nd German edition.

21. L. Cremona. *Le Figure Reciproche Nella Statica Grafica* (Milan, 1872). Translated into French by Bossut (G.-V., 1885).

22. *Elementi di Calcolo Grafico* (Turin, Paravia, 1874).

23. M. Lévy. *La Statique Graphique et ses Applications aux Constructions* (Paris, G.-V., 1874). A 2nd edition, in four volumes rather than one, was produced in the period 1886–1888.

24. J. Massau. *Mémoire sur l'Intégration Graphique et ses Applications*. Published as a single volume after first having appeared in installements (1878 to 1890) in *Ann. des Ing. Sortis des Écoles Spéc. de Gand.*

25. A Favaro. *Calcul Graphique*. Volume II, *Lecons de Statique Graphique*, translated with appendixes and notes by P. Terrier (Paris, G.-V., 1885).

26. E. Rouché. *Cours de Statique Graphique Professé au Conservatoire des Arts et Métiers.* Incorporated as part of the *Encyclopédie des Travaux Publics* (Paris, G.-V., 1889).

27. C. Runge. *Graphical Methods* (New York, Columbia University Press, 1912).

Grapho-Mechanical Calculation

(See also entry 15.)

28. B. Abdank-Abakanowicz. *Les Intégraphes* (G.-V., 1886).

29. H. de Morin *Les Appareils d'Intégration* (G.-V., 1893).

30. E. Pascal. *I Miei Integrafi per Equazioni Differenziali* (Naples, 1914).

Nomographic Calculation

(See also the works listed in the endnotes for Chapter IV and entries 24 and 27.)

31. L. Pouchet. *Arithmétique Linéaire*. An appendix to the work *Métrologie Terrestre* (Rouen, 1797).

32. L. Lalanne. *Mémoire sur les Tables Graphiques et la Géométrie Anamorphique* (*A.P.C.*, first Part, 1846).

33. Ch. Lallemand. *Les Abaques Hexagonaux* (manuscript, 1885).

34. E. Goedseels. *Les Procédés pour Simplifier le Calcul . . .* (Brussels, Lagaert, 1898).

35. R. Soreau. *Contribution à la Théorie et aux Applications de la Nomographie* (*Soc. des Ing. Civils*, 1901).

36. R. Soreau. *Nomographie. Théorie des Abaques* (Paris, Chiron, 1921).

37. N. Gercevanoff. *The Principles of Nomographic Calculation and Their Application to Graphical Integration* (in Russian) (Saint Petersburg, 1906).

38. J. Clark. *Théorie Génerale des Abaques d'Alignement* (*Rev. de Méc.*, 1907).

Nomo-Mechanical Calculation

(See also entry 15.)

39. L. Torres Quevedo. *Machines à Calculer* (*Mémoires Présentés par Divers Savants à l'Académie des Sciences*, Vol. XXXII, Number 9, 1901).

Notes

1. Where there have been several editors of a work, the reference is always to the most recent.

2. (Ed.) d'Ocagne identified the publisher as "Spa."

3. (Ed.) This work is reproduced as Vol. 2 in the Charles Babbage Institute Reprint Series for the History of Computing.

Index of Names and Major Ideas, Machines, and Inventions